Cove

SAND IN MY SHOES
Wartime Diaries of a WAAF

SAND IN
MY SHOES

Wartime Diaries of a WAAF

Joan Rice

Harper*Press*
An Imprint of HarperCollins*Publishers*

Harper*Press*
An imprint of HarperCollins*Publishers*
77–85 Fulham Palace Road,
Hammersmith, London W6 8JB

www.harpercollins.co.uk

Published by HarperCollins*Publishers* 2006
1

A catalogue record for this book
is available from the British Library

HB ISBN-13 978-0-00-722820-1
HB ISBN-10 0-00-722820-1

TPB ISBN-13 978-0-00-724393-8
TPB ISBN-10 0-00-724393-6

Set in Times by
Rowland Phototypesetting Ltd, Bury St Edmunds, Suffolk

Printed and bound in Great Britain by
Clays Ltd, St Ives plc

In memory of Hugh,
my husband of forty-six years.

And in memory also of those
young Hurricane pilots of 504 Squadron
who fought so bravely in the Battle of Britain.

SAND IN MY SHOES
(Frank Loesser/Victor Schertzinger)

Sand in my shoes, sand from Havana
Calling me to that ever so heavenly shore
Calling me back to you once more
Dreams in the night, dreams of Havana
Dreams of a love I hadn't the strength to refuse
Darling the sand is in my shoes
Deep in my veins the sensuous strains
Of the soft guitar
Deep in my soul the thunderous roll
Of a tropic sea under the stars,
That was Havana
You are the moonlit mem'ry I can't seem to lose
That's why my life's an endless cruise
All that is real is the feel of the sand in my shoes

(Instrumental Interlude)

Deep in my veins the sensuous strains
Of the soft guitar
Deep in my soul the thunderous roll
Of a tropic sea under the stars,
That was Havana
You are the moonlit mem'ry I can't seem to lose
That's why my life's and endless cruise
All that is real is the feel of the sand in my shoes
Sand in my shoes
Sand from Havana.

CONTENTS

FOREWORD

When Mother asked if we thought it would be a good thing to type out her war diary for the family to read, we politely said yes. We assumed there would be no real heroics in there, but we did not really know what Mother had done in the war (apart from get married in Cairo – oops! I've given away the ending) so we did not quite know what to expect. And even though we knew that Mother was a good writer, we did not expect anything like this.

For those of us lucky enough to be born after the end of what proved to be the last World War of the twentieth century, 1939 is beyond our imagination. L.P. Hartley's description of the past as 'a foreign country' is not powerful enough: for those of us who have been civilians all our lives, those war years are a different world. We grew up in the shadow of war, maybe, but it never became a reality. We never had it so good, as Harold Macmillan never said.

My parents were among those unlucky ones who were of a generation who had to fight. But, to read their diaries, we might feel that in many ways they were the lucky ones. As my mother's diary makes very clear, she enjoyed the war most of the time, 'Never in my life have my days been so round and so snug,' she writes in 1940, 'and this is a war, a clash of civilization. It is odd.' For my brothers and me, my parents' war experiences were crucial, because without the upheaval that Hitler caused, my father and mother would never have met, and we – my brothers, our children and our grandchildren – would not be here. We are not unique, of course: there are millions of us all over Europe, America and elsewhere who owe their existence to Hitler's decision to invade Poland in September 1939. No wonder Europe was entirely reshaped by the war, and not just in terms of national borders traced on maps. Hitler's pursuit of his belief in the ideal of a Master Race proved to be an Orwellian reality, probably resulting in a greater mongrelization of Europe than any other single event in history. I am proud to be one of those mongrels.

It is a very strange sensation to read the diary of your mother, especially when it deals with the time before you existed. In many ways, the person revealed in this diary is a stranger, a woman who happens to have the same name as my mother. If I didn't know it was Mother who had written it, I would never have guessed. When we were growing up, I never noticed the determination and ambition that are revealed in the diary, never thought of Mother as a person who had ever scored three goals in a hockey match, or who actually enjoyed gardening, or who ever smoked. Yet here it is, a true picture of the young woman who, within seven years of finishing her diary, would be mistress of a vast crumbling farmhouse with three sons rushing around her feet. I never remember her remarking, as she does in the diary, 'Housework is nothing like as soul-destroying as typing.' But I am still worried about the entry for 31 March 1941. She was in hospital, sharing a ward with 'thirty bawling brats', an experience which, she writes, 'has soured me as a confirmed child hater.' Not the person I know.

Mother's ambition to be a writer was the one thing that never flagged. I remember throughout our childhood hearing the clatter of the typewriter as Mother somehow found time between school runs, dog walking and keeping Popefield Farm in some sort of order, to write another short story, or a piece for *Woman's Hour* or *Punch*. It seemed to us quite natural that a person could earn money from writing and broadcasting, because Mother did. She never had time to write that epic novel, for which the three of us must be largely to blame, but she was a good and regularly published writer. We all, to a greater or lesser extent, have followed her example.

Neither of my parents were ever remotely military people. They never spoke about their war experiences, except to tell us of their wedding day or self-deprecatory anecdotes about why Father never won the M.C. or about his German measles in the invasion of Sicily. We found it odd (as did Father) that his tailor persisted in addressing him as Major Rice over a decade after the war had ended and he had been demobbed, and it has only really occurred to me now, on re-reading the diaries, that none of my parents' wartime colleagues became friends after the war. I do not think I ever met any of the people mentioned in the diary, apart from those that Mother knew from before the war and with whom she remained

xiii

friends for years, in one case to this day. The war was a break in existence, and it was clearly one they were both eager to put behind them as soon as it was all over.

I also have to keep reminding myself how young Mother was when the war began. It was only a fortnight or so after her 20th birthday. I was at university on my 20th birthday, the extent of my worries being which pub to celebrate in. When she went to view the Blitz damage in Kilburn, she noted one shop, 'where I used to buy my school hats', which hadn't a window left. She would have been buying her school hats there only three or four years earlier. It must have been terrifying to be part of 'a generation without a tomorrow, alive and beautiful in our lovely today.'

On board a ship to Egypt, aged 22 and a half, she gets into a deep discussion about the state of the world, and notes, 'it's a dreadful and depressing thing if the men with ideals and intelligence are already so disillusioned that they will not even fight for the future. And then Diana came over, and Roger, and we played a game of deck quoits.' The answer to everything when you are 22, a game of deck quoits.

Jonathan Rice
January 2006

INTRODUCTION

In 1939 I was nineteen years old, living with my parents in the small Surrey village of Claygate. We had a detached house, a largish garden, a car in the garage. Our comparative prosperity was a recent event; my parents, whose financial highs and lows had punctuated my childhood, had found themselves three years earlier on a high. I was now a typical middle-class unmarried daughter. I had left school at just seventeen with matriculation. No thoughts of higher education were considered. Universities were not an option for girls except for the brilliant few or those with wealthy parents who did not consider a university education a waste of time for their daughters.

Like many of my contemporaries I went to a secretarial college and from there to a job as a shorthand typist. I was considered to be one of the lucky ones. I was taken on by the Asiatic Petroleum Company (Shell) which – according to the principal of my college – chose only the cream of the cream. As the cream we were paid top salaries, £2 10s (old money) a week as opposed to the £2 paid by the next most desirable firm – ICI.[1] My fellow typists in Bitumen, the department to which I was

---

[1] Imperial Chemical Industries plc.

assigned, were a pleasant lot; the work, if boring as far as I was concerned, was far from arduous and the attitude of Shell towards its female staff was positively paternal. We might have to wear a uniform provided free by the firm – navy-blue serge in winter, beige shantung in summer – until we reached the rank of senior secretary, but unlike the men and almost everyone else in those days, we did not have to work on Saturday mornings.

There was a staff canteen where we were provided free with morning coffee and afternoon tea, and an excellent lunch at bargain prices. On Fridays, just before pay day, a satisfying dish of chips and peas and lashings of gravy could be bought for five (old) pence. Our leisure hours were equally well catered for. On the river at Teddington near where I lived was Lensbury, the firm's palatial sports club where just about every sport was provided for and where there were weekly dances. In Claygate itself there was a tennis club and an amateur dramatic society. Nearby Richmond had an ice-skating rink. The cinema was a walk across the common to Esher. I had a bicycle; I was learning to drive. It was the sort of life most girls of my class were contented with until they were married.

I wanted to get married, of course, since the alternative was to end up a despised spinster like the head of our typing pool, an old woman of forty, pitied and mocked by us younger girls. In my depressed moments I saw that as being my fate. I was not a success with my male contemporaries. However hard I tried to conform to the then social climate where men called all the shots, they seemed to sense that I was different in an undesirable way. My ambitions were not the ambitions of my contemporaries. I wanted to write; I wanted to travel; I wanted to be famous. But all I got were rejection slips from editors, and how could I save up for a world trip on £2 10s a week? Then, in September 1939, war was declared. This was my opportunity, I seized it immediately. I joined the Women's Auxiliary Air Force (WAAF).

This diary covers the years from September 1939 to December 1942, by which time I was engaged. Thereafter until the end of the war if I wanted to write up any goings on, I did so in letters to my fiancé, later my husband.

For the first eighteen months of the war I was posted to the RAF Station, Hendon as a secretary, progressing from ACW2[2] to corporal, and where the so-called 'phoney war' eventually gave way to the Battle of Britain and the bombing of London. RAF Station Hendon also had its share of air raids during this period.

In May 1941 I was commissioned and posted to RAF Medmenham as a photographic interpreter.[3] This, for me, was the least enjoyable period of my WAAF career, but it led in January 1942 to an overseas posting to Egypt. There I remained for two years, except for an interlude when the WAAF members of our unit were evacuated to what was then Palestine. (We owed this abrupt departure

[2] Aircraft Woman 2nd Class.
[3] Photographs of enemy territory were taken, brought back and examined for any relevant information.

to General Rommel and his army who had come danger-ously near to occupying Cairo.) In this, final section I have included excerpts from my husband's own diary.

In January 1944 I was given a compassionate posting back to England. My husband, after service with the Eighth Army through the desert, Sicily and Italy, had also returned home to join the preparations for the Second Front. As a result I became pregnant and left the WAAF in the summer of 1944. In November that year the first of our three sons[4] was born.

Joan Rice

[4] 1944 Sir Tim Rice. Lyricist, author and broadcaster
1947 Jonathan Rice. Author, broadcaster and lecturer
1950 Andrew Rice. Advertising guru (South Africa) and broad-caster

PART I

Hendon,
The Phoney War

1939

20 September 1939

I'm a member now of the WAAF but I must begin from the beginning. On Tuesday afternoon I went along to Ariel House, Strand, to see if I could be enrolled. A few of my particulars were taken and I was told to wait until the recruiting officer could see me. I sat on a bench with a lot of other women and the hours went by. After long ages she did see me, looking very snappy with red hair and the Air Force uniform which, barring the awful shoes and stockings, is quite good. She talked a lot about did I know what I was doing and service discipline, and saying they wanted people badly at Hendon with good shorthand and typing, then sent me to another woman to fill in a form. That done I was told to return for the medical exam this morning. I have passed and am now in the RAF. I begin with 2s 3d a day in contrast to those not on special duties who only get 1s 4d, and I may (I hope) have to go abroad. I am now waiting to be called up to Hendon.

I'll explain my reasons for joining. Firstly, doing one's bit. I suppose that's there, though it doesn't seem particularly in evidence at the moment. Secondly, this life will get me away from home, make me adult and independent. Thirdly, it's a change and adventure. Fourthly and at the present most strongly, I want to swank around in a uniform.

I had lunch with Mother at the Bolivar today. There were girls, smart and sophisticated, drinking with men at the bar. I felt about fifteen. I want to be able to be at any time at ease, with poise and sophistication. I hope this new life will help me. It will be experience. Sitting in Claygate isn't going to teach me about life. The WAAF should. When the war is over I want to be fully equipped to go back immediately to my goal of successful writer. If I'm alive and there's any civilisation alive, I'll do it. Meantime this diary goes with me to Hendon.

8 October 1939

I am sitting on Betty's[1] bed (a Shell colleague, now living with my parents). Opposite on my own is a pile of belongings and a far too small suitcase. Herewith the events leading up to my last day at home (excuse legal phrasing but I have just returned from making my will). I look at my packing and have the same sick and 'wish I hadn't done it' feeling in my tummy that was there on going back to the convent (boarding school) evenings. Only tonight have I realised that I'm going into this new

[1] Betty Ross, who lived with my parents as a paying guest when Shell was evacuated.

unknown living. Even at Bunty's[2] (a school friend with whom I had been staying), when she and her mother made up absurd adventures about me in the Air Force which ended with me dropping from the air onto a submarine, and much laughter in which I joined, it was impossibly far away. Even when Mother phoned and said I was to go on Monday it was still impossible to happen. Now it is my last night at home and no one but you must know how I feel or I'd probably cry. Because of that it's going to be good for me. I've got to be adult. I've got to be self-assured. I've got to be able to go anywhere and not be shy. At least I'll have you with me.

9 October 1939

First Day in the life of a WAAF. It began with rain and nearly missing the train at Claygate; more rain, heavy bags and misery in the Strand; more rain, going the wrong way and arriving late at Hendon. Soaked and surly I filled in a 'history sheet' and went in the rain to my billet which is, or rather are, the old married quarters of the RAF. After that we went up to get our equipment which at the moment consists of one oversized raincoat and a service gas mask. Then we had to walk in the rain to the aerodrome to be vaccinated by a very large, very silent, very alluring doctor. Next the lunch, a dubious stew and a paper piece of tart eaten on one plate and a tin-topped

---

[2] Bunty Goldie, now Bunty Jackman – the only person from the diaries who has remained a friend.

table. After that a gas lecture and a mask demonstration. Next tea, a fish cake and bread and jam, and then *à la liberté*.

I have managed to cultivate a friendship with a girl called Joyce[3] who has a car and we went out on a voyage of shopping and discovery. We discovered little except that the car wouldn't go and spent most of the time pushing it. Coming home I put on slacks and the rest of our house mates came in – the NCO[4] (a nice girl called Mike) and a girl called Scotty with a squashed-in face – and we drank tea and listened to them talking. I must go to bed now. It's heroic writing this.

15 October 1939

It's unbelievable that to go from Hendon to home all that needs to be done is a short train journey. The two worlds are so much further apart than a journey through a wasteland; howling wind and outer darkness seems fitting to bridge the gap. Even now at home this evening I belong here no longer. I should have had my leave from Sunday night to Monday night, but on Saturday evening I learnt that I'm to be transferred to Ruislip tomorrow and so was allowed home before the change. I'm lucky to get a permanent job so quickly. Hendon is a training centre for the WAAF and most people are there longer than I've been. The thing I've hated most about Hendon

[3] Joyce Davidge.
[4] Non-Commissioned Officer.

6

is having no definite work but hanging around a crowded orderly room all day with nothing to do and everybody looking at you as if you should be busy. In fact, had I written this up last Tuesday (can I possibly have been in the Air Force only six days?), I would have reflected on the deepest depths of despair to which the human soul can reach. I was so miserable I could no longer think nor reason, just move in a fog of despondence. Fortunately misery cannot go on being misery eternally (that's why hell's such a dumb idea), and my emotions rose until now, when I'm glad that while the war is on I'm in the WAAF.

After this war I might be quite well off. Shell are saving one pound a week for me for the duration in addition to my Provident fund (staff who volunteered for war work were still considered as employed by Shell), and I've heard that we may get gratuities at the end of the war. I'll have to go back to Shell for a bit for decency's sake and then Heigh Ho for the world and adventure. I haven't told you yet all about life in the WAAF but I'm going to have a bath and will maybe write more later.

(Much later in the afternoon. Raining and raining and raining outside and us all in warm before the fire.) We light a fire in the downstairs room and sit around it, singing sometimes with a girl called Renee,[5] just back from Germany, playing the accordion, and sometimes talking and going one by one to the bath if we have

---

[5] Renee Bedell – who had been working for the British Council.

managed to coax the boiler into a blaze. I like all the girls in our house except the one called Scotty who unfortunately is in the same bedroom as me. I think there's something wrong about her. I've heard Mickey[6] and Joyce talking about it but they won't tell me. I must look innocent. It's very annoying.

The working part of the day is, as I've said, foul (I am a trained secretary) but you can get out of most of it by going to games and drill. The food is really quite good if the way of eating it very primitive. I shudder to think of my table manners when this war is over, but I shall be tough what with marching, early rises and hard beds. They have some very good cheap cinema shows in the aeroplane hangars, concerts for the troops and games in the evening like fencing and badminton.

16 October 1939

Would you believe it? After all I'm not being moved. When I got back from leave yesterday I was told that the commanding officer wanted me to stay, and Frances (our NCO) told me kindly that she likes to hang on to efficient people. Well, I'm all for it. I like it here now. I like my billet companions except the before-mentioned Scotty, but there's hope she'll be going soon. I like the free concerts and cheap cinemas and railway service tickets, and the coming glory of a uniform and being different to

[6] Mickey Johnston.

the herd. I've also heard there's a library on the Station and that a hairdresser has been installed to shampoo and set for 1s 6d a time.

I'm all for the RAF. I'm beginning to be proud of the company and myself and spent the evening polishing my shoes, washing my stockings and pressing my mac. I like most of all being independent. (I mean free from the bondage of a life at home that there must be in the best of them. You can't grow up till you leave your parents. I know that now.)

I'm sitting writing this before the fire, waiting till Pat finishes with the bath. Upstairs Mike and Frances and Mickey are cleaning their rooms in readiness for to-morrow's billet inspection, and I've just heard them say that another lot of propaganda pamphlets went off from here to Germany today. Despite events like that though you might be miles away from any war here – there's no time to talk about it. Ah ha, this diary now contains a STATE SECRET.

19 October 1939

We had a concert tonight over in one of the furthest aeroplane hangars, and the first half was broadcast as from 'Somewhere in England'. A great many photographs were taken of the female artists with the RAF and the male artists with the WAAF, and also numerous news-reels. As I was unfortunately at the back of the hall I doubt if my bright camera-smiling face will flash over England. In the interval Joyce and I pushed our way

through the mob and got Will Hay to autograph our pro-
grammes. The programme was too long and somewhat
patchy, the community singing being the best, especially
our rendering of 'I'll See You Again' and 'Tipperary'
which always makes me want to cry.

We marched back in the dark with Ely (an NCO)
running up and down the long, long line shouting at us
to keep in step and not hold hands and not talk and not
sing, and then at the gate being nice again and saying
'Goodnight – sleep well'. Now we're sitting in our bedroom in various stages of night attire and translating one
of the German pamphlets illegally obtained and feeling
like we're having a secret meeting.

20 October 1939 (early in the morning before
reporting for duty)

The night before last the Special Police on the aerodrome gave a dance and forty of the WAAFs, which
included all our house except Mickey Johnston, went to
it. It was pretty putrid really, the most oafish soldiers, and
while Mike, Joyce and Scotty got lifts home, Pat and I
came home with a frightful soldier, very fresh, whom we
just couldn't shake off. Renee was sitting on the doorstep
waiting for us and Mike had the late pass key! After
waiting in the cold for about twenty minutes and calling
Mike every name we could think of (my vocabulary has
increased considerably since living here), we broke in the
back window and made hay with Mike's bed and removed
her pyjama cord. With that and other things we didn't get

to bed till well after twelve and had to be up at some ungodly hour.

Last night I accepted the invitation of the girl next door but one to go fencing with her, but after a long windy walk across the aerodrome we found the instructor wasn't there. However, she took me back and gave me hot soup and we made plans for our lives after the war. I'm never, never going back to shorthand typing. I'm going to Prague, probably to work in the British Institute and write the rest of the day. Mickey did that and will show me the ropes.

23 October 1939

I was ill with a cold all day Sunday after a horrible night upstairs sleeping with Mike as I just couldn't face a night alone with Scotty (Joyce being on leave). The day was pleasant with a continual string of visitors in the morning, tea and coffee and biscuits and books, and an afternoon almost asleep with the sun through the open window, and outside in the garden Renee and Deirdre gardening and laughing at Deirdre's jokes; and then in the evening Mike and Frances buying me chocolate and buns to supplement the invalid diet. Today, by a little push and a kindly fate, I snitched from a more senior typist an all-day job for the deputy commander and worked away at it voluntarily till 7.30 on the reasoning that nothing done for the Powers on High is wasted. It was a list of the girls to be posted permanently to Hendon and we – Frances, Mike, Joyce, Mickey and I are on it and SCOTTY IS NOT. If you know Scotty who smells and doesn't wash and who is loud, man-mad and crude you would understand our rejoicings. We've made wonderful plans for transforming our house when she's gone, washing it out and bringing comforts from home. I am so happy here now – it's a wonderful life.

29 October 1939

Sitting before the fire in the lounge, home on forty-eight hours' leave, a summary of thoughts and events seems appropriate. As the first is always easier I'll start with that and hope that the events will fit themselves in as I go along.

Why I like the RAF. I like having no responsibilities. I like not having to worry about clothes and food and money, and what I am to do next. With all that taken care of and enough for me to do to keep me from being lazy, my brain can give all of its time to its work and here I am positively popping with ideas, and I prefer the ideas. Fortunately both Mickey and Frances write and when Scotty's gone (she goes Monday!) we shall have the downstairs bedroom for a living room and the little upstairs one for us three to retire and work in. Leaving this 'no outside worry' way of living to come home has unsettled me. I didn't want to hear how business is bad and how my mother had cried one night missing me. When this war's over I'm going away. I'm never being in a safe job again, and she'll not want it and perhaps they'll be poor and Shell will be a safe steady job. I won't stay. When this war's over, diary, I swear I'll be writing you in the capitals of Europe and the stranger places of the world, but I want not to have to feel guilty about it.

31 October 1939

It hasn't been the best of weeks. It began with my returning from leave not to a cheery household, but to a place so strangely deserted that I thought it was another *Marie Celeste*. I undressed before a fire someone else had lit, bathed in water someone else had heated, and stared at a half-finished cigarette someone else had smoked and all the while in an empty house. They returned in dribbles, Mike tired and touchy so that we all had to be careful with her for the evening, and Renee bossy and irritating. Since then the house has been parted by a pro Renee and a pro Frances battle over a girl called Reynolds whom Renee has foisted on No. 7 Booth Road.

Last night Joyce and I had an orgy of cleaning to get our room clean now that Scotty has gone (plus, we fear, my blue hairbrush and Joyce's mascot monkey). While Renee spoke German to Mickey so that we couldn't understand and giggled, I scrubbed the floor and Joyce polished it, and between us we got the room immaculate. I like Joyce. She's plump with bright yellow hair and feet that look most attractive from behind when she walks.

I'm very tired. Hence the low level of this entry of squabbling women is neither ennobling nor uplifting but positively fourth form. I must go and have a bath.

13

7 November 1939

I ought to tell you about the church parade on Sunday and the press photographers and Gaumont British News taking newsreels and photographs of us today, but I've got to report back for afternoon duty in about five minutes and while I write this our NCO is lamenting about the untidiness of the house. Really, living in this whirl of publicity it's going to be hard being nobody when the war's over.

8 November 1939

Last night a good time was had by all. Six of us went to a cinema at Hendon and saw an excellent French film called *Drame de Shanghai*. After the film we stumbled through the blackout to a restaurant where we ate frankfurter sausages and sauerkraut and laughed immoderately. On our return, Joyce's car refused to go and after pushing it miles down roads assisted by taxi drivers and pursued by buses the other four went home to sign us in before 9.30, leaving Joyce and me to park the car in the Hendon Way and walk across half the aerodrome to the MT[7] sheds and a driver Joyce knew who would retrieve and mend it for her. It was a wonderful walk – stars and a clear sky and the wind in our hair. Joyce and I are trying to get out of our present house for one where we can

[7] Motor Transport.

have a room to ourselves and a little less of this hearty communal living.

9 November 1939

Owing to the pleasing fact that all surplus No. 11 Company WAAF are being posted away from Hendon at a great rate, our previous billet, No. 7 Booth Road, was formally condemned and Joyce and I this evening moved into the top bedroom of No. 18. After No. 7, where every time you put the blackout down, part of the wall falls with it and where our bedroom was like trying to live and sleep on a dirty, busy railway platform, this is the Ritz Hotel.

We have a large room intended for three but which we trust to keep exclusively to ourselves, and now we have got it straight we have to keep on looking to believe it's true. One thing it lacked was a table. Remembering that No. 7 was condemned anyway we decided that we, as well as anyone else, might as well enjoy the pickings. With this in mind Joyce and I carried out the table under cover of the blackout down Booth Road, but even in a blackout a table is not easy to disguise. We were caught on our new doorstep by Johnston, one of the girls downstairs, but were able to laugh it off airily and take it upstairs, without removing any great part of the staircase wall, where it now rests, very fetching with our wireless on it.

Later in the evening Joyce returned to collect the last of her luggage from No. 7, while I washed and scrubbed in the bath. Frances and Mike and some chaps had returned from the cinema and cried angrily about the missing table. Joyce not only denied stealing it but questioned a justly indignant Mickey about its disappearance. She was about to depart when Frances asked if she could come round in the morning and see what sort of room we'd got. 'Yes,' said Joyce, turning a little blue. The table is very large and very obvious. The situation is not what I'd call happy.

13 November 1939

Coming back here from leave I was told that breakfast had been changed from the ladylike hour of eight to the grey and 'still a few stars' time of 7.15 in order that we may come back later and clean up our respective houses. Still, in compensation, the WAAFs themselves have taken over the cooking completely and everything now is cleaned and better and – excess of refinement – we have flowers on the tables.

15 November 1939

Coming back in the Tube, an overheard dialogue:

'What's she?' (I had my uniform on, at least all of it I've got which includes a hat.)

'Oh' – contemptuously – 'Fire Service.' (Me sitting there with 'RAF' bang in the middle of my uniform.)

'Why don't you join it?'

'They only take all those society and titled people.'

Visible attempt from me to look society and titled.

20 November 1939

On Saturday Joyce and I and two other girls got given tickets for an ice hockey match at Wembley. We had simply super seats and enjoyed ourselves greatly, eating a great quantity of miscellaneous food and cheering immoderately. At about ten we left to see our home bus disappearing into the blackout. After forty minutes of waiting in the rain we were glad to see the next bus, so judge our disgust when the conductor told us that the last bus right through to Colindale went at eight o'clock A.M. After another wait we got a train to Wembley Park, and after a still longer wait in still heavier rain for a non-existent bus we had to take a taxi back: not very kind on my slight finances. We had to be in by twelve as there had been a hell of a stink the night before when five WAAF came in at five in the morning from a night out at the Kit Kat Club with those forbidden gods, the officers.

Yesterday everybody else in the house was out so I lit a fire, ate a lot, went to bed with a bottle and listened in the darkness to *The Thin Man* on our wireless, and then slept until woken up by Joyce dropping her Optrex bottle at one o'clock in the morning. On the bottom of her bed was a pile of books brought from her home, all of them asking that I read them, and I'm starting tonight on Clement Dane's *Will Shakespeare*.

Tomorrow, those of us who were posted to Hendon move over to work at Station Headquarters, I with the job I've been hoping for: secretary to the Commanding Officer (CO), Mrs Rowley – small, dark, handsome, immaculate, sensible, intelligent, fair and so many things so few women ever are. Today I went up and collected my anti-gas clothing which consists of a five-times-too-large coat and a colossal hat. In all this, plus goggles and gas mask, I certainly shan't die of a gas attack. I'll be suffocated long before that.

25 November 1939

One day last week in the inevitable rain I went over to Bunty's on late leave pass. My hat had been borrowed by another WAAF – twelve of us had been chosen to take part in a Tommy Trinder[8] film and between us we had pooled our uniform resources to equip them credit-ably – and I arrived untidy, dirty and shabby but full of such confidence that neither clothes nor looks mattered at all.

I ate enormously, had a bath there by torch light as of course the Goldies[9] had not got proper blackout curtains, and cleaner but with hair even more untidy went back to laugh and talk with Bunty, Bernie and Eric[10] with such effect that Eric took me back as far as King's Cross. Sitting beside him in an empty Tube carriage and laughing with him over a coffee at King's Cross Station I tried to remember that a 'to-be-remembered' moment was

[8] A popular comedian of the time.
[9] Bunty's parents.
[10] Bernie and Eric were two friends of Bunty's; they all met at the Goldies' tennis club.

happening and that I must savour it fully, but the time went on and then I was waving him goodbye, and when I was back at Hendon it was unreal and unhappenable. I wish I got these moods of get anything and confidence more often. When they come nothing can stop me. When I really want a thing it always happens.

I've had my first promotion in the WAAF. I was reclassified on Thursday to ACW1[11] from ACW2 and get, I think, sixpence more a day. I also went to Moss Bros today and ordered a second uniform (the first, I may say, is still to be issued to me), Mother having advanced me the money. I'm being fitted on Friday and it should be ready for me in ten days. I've optimistically and illegally had it made in officer's cloth.

29 November 1939

Such goings on. A girl called Single, known as Boompsie, who works over with 24 Squadron was in a room full of officers and who walked in but DAVID NIVEN, yes, really and truly, cross Single's fat heart. Single, needless to say, sat on immovable, to the surprise of her officer who had now finished with her, and looked and looked at the divine apparition. Rumour has it that he wants to join the RAF and still wilder rumour that he will be posted here. As a result WAAFs no longer go around as God made them, lanky hair, shining face and

[11] Aircraft Woman 1st Class.

much dirt but have polished and pushed themselves into their pre-war shapes.

A further story re David Niven comes from Ghisi, the girl downstairs in our new house. She got the message that a Mr Niven was arriving today and please arrange transport. Ghisi arranged and Mr Niven arrived. Ghisi looked at him and left the room. Outside a cackle of officers informed her it was DAVID NIVEN. Back rushed Ghisi to hear an also unsuspecting squadron leader telling poor Mr Niven that all the transport she had been able to arrange was a Singer van. Seeing the van Mr Niven murmured faintly he'd get a taxi. 'Well,' said the squadron leader heartily, ignoring Ghisi's 'It's the film star' in sign language behind his back, 'get one from Hendon, not Golders Green. It's 2 shillings cheaper.'

This evening I have battled with fire. I lit the bedroom fire five times and the boiler three and conquered them both. I must be like those odd natives with the gift of chucking live fire about. I can now pick up and carry smoking coals without inconvenience. I also used the two inside pages of Ray Atkinson's *Daily Telegraph* but will be in bed and asleep before she returns.

5 December 1939

Joyce is sitting on the floor with her feet in our beastly little fire which is sulking because I've made it burn, reading half aloud Clement Dane's *Will Shakespeare* and being anxious because she's forgetting how to act. I am lying on the bed in my issued vest and pants, a jumper, slacks, a cardigan, and a dressing gown and am only just warm.

Last night both of us went to an airmen's dance way down in East Camp and had a very good time, meeting up again only when it was time to return, I feeling especially lucky in finding a North Country airman who could actually dance. We got in about one o'clock and consequently feel more than a little jaded now, especially after the perfectly beastly day. Our dearly beloved, our cherished Mrs Rowley has left us to go to Air Ministry. There's a faint hope that she may only be attached and not posted but it's too dim to comfort our desolate souls. I was surprised to find how much people had been jealous of me working for her and being made an ACW1. One girl (aren't women delightful en bloc?) went so far as to tell me that I was through and would be shipped to West Drayton without delay. West Drayton to the WAAF is what the most dreaded German concentration camp is to a Jew.[12] Fortunately I am still well installed here and shall go on working for whoever is our next CO but I shall miss Mrs Rowley.

You remember Eric who brought me home from King's Cross? When I was over at Bunty's on Sunday she told me that he had urgently phoned her up for my address and was much smitten.

---

[12] By this time we had heard quite a bit about the existence of concentration camps within Germany. In 1938–9 there was a stream of refugees from Germany to the UK, mostly children, few of whom ever saw their parents again.

8 December 1939

Yesterday I had a letter from Eric – a very nice letter asking me to choose any show I liked for Tuesday night and that he'd take me. I've chosen *Black Velvet*, I will have my uniform and, as Bunty says he's very generous, I should enjoy myself greatly. I am not in the least in love with him but like him very much. I'll tell you about it Tuesday.

11 December 1939

I'm sitting before our fire, throwing out heat for once, having just finished a violent spring-clean of the room. Monday evening is the only time it gets any attention, Tuesday being an inspection. We both of us get up too late other days to do anything but get ourselves to work on time.

Having forgotten to buy any flowers and there being no more in the gardens to steal I've piled four oranges and an apple on a plate for ornament and feel I owe it to the room not to eat them. Sitting where I am I fortunately can't see them.

I wrote to Eric on Friday saying would he 'phone me over the weekend to arrange a meeting'. He didn't and there's been no word today. I'm resigned now to it having been an illusion, an unreal impossible dream, but oh dear I would so have liked to have gone.

14 December 1939

Having heard me say that I was going visit-making up the road, our beastly little fire is burning with wildest abandon, intent obvious – to be out before my return. Incidentally, how does it manage to burn a whole evening and not heat the room a single degree?

I went out with Eric after all on Tuesday. He hadn't been able to phone because of our telephone being out of order. Bunty and Bernie came too and it was quite enjoyable, but I saw him without the glamour of the rain and the wind and my own laughing abandon, and he's a very ordinary boy.

Last night Joyce and I and her car, behaving itself for once, went to the pictures, smoking ourselves silly, and then coming back, spreading her rug before the fire and eating chips and my sponge cake from home, oranges and the last of Eric's chocolates, and I enjoying myself far more than the night before. We certainly are pampered in the WAAF. In addition to all MT drivers being forbidden to drive anything heavier than 15 cwt and no one allowed to work after four o'clock, we are to have masses of new equipment including still-expected snappy sports suits, TWO uniforms, brushes, combs and towels. The taxpayers are certainly doing us proud.

21 December 1939

Last night Joyce and I had a party. First I drank cider and then I drank gin and lime and then a concoction of

Joyce's called Black Velvet and then gin and lime, and then I would have had a glass of sherry except that after two mouthfuls, swallowed in my urgent desire for the experience of drunkenness, Joyce drank the rest for me. I began to get very tired and just couldn't wake up to say goodbye when our guests went, and then the next thing I knew was that strange hands, e.g. Dillon and Firebrace, whose passes extended beyond ten o'clock, were undressing me. I endeavoured to sit up and protest against this outrage but they were both so much stronger than me that the rest of my clothes, to an accompaniment of soothing and infuriating murmurs, were taken from me. I got up a little later and was sick and then despite my shrieks that I wouldn't go to bed I was thrust into the blankets, given a bottle and then ignored when I wanted to talk with them.

Today, chastened and sick in my stomach, I have been the centre of indulgent amusement, and sat tonight pensively sipping a very weak brandy and soda recommended to soothe my stomach in front of the downstairs room fire, feeling that, as an experience, once is enough of getting drunk.

25 December 1939

They let us have breakfast at half past eight, a very nice breakfast of Cornflakes, ham, hot rolls and coffee, and afterwards numerous people came along to our billet bringing with them cakes and fruit and nuts and chocolate and even a wireless and we huddled round the downstairs fire sipping sherry, eating oddments and talking. Lunch was excellent – the inevitable turkey and Christmas pudding with nuts and fruit and beer – and our officers and sergeants to wait on us.[13] After lunch we repeated the morning's huddle round the fire till, at 6.30, we got ourselves out of our slacks and into reasonable clothes for the concert. It was an appalling concert but the airmen behind us were so amusing we laughed ourselves sick.

After the concert came a social at the NAAFI[14] for airmen and airwomen which we were all enjoying when the group captain removed the snarling WAAFs at eleven o'clock. From 11.30 to one o'clock we again sat round the fire eating and talking and so ended my first Christmas Day.

---

[13] Officers waiting on other ranks is still the custom in the Armed Forces on Christmas Day.
[14] The Navy, Army and Air Force Institute runs shops and clubs for the Armed Forces, and then gives its profits back to the Services.

Events of 1939

1 September Germany invaded Poland without a declaration of war.

3 September Britain and France declared war on Germany.

27 September Warsaw surrendered to the Nazis.

29 September National registration was carried out in the UK to supply the entire population with Identity Cards.

14 October HMS *Royal Oak* was sunk at port in Scapa Flow by a German U-boat; 833 men died in Britain's first heavy loss.

21 October Conscription began of men aged between twenty and twenty-three.

28 October The first German plane was shot down over Great Britain.

8 November A failed attempt to assassinate Hitler killed nine people in Munich.

30 November The Red Army marched into Finland.

1940

7 January 1940

Joyce and I have pulled the beds around the fire, stolen the pouffe from Peggy's bed downstairs, unpouffed it and spread it around the ground for us to loll against. On the beds are books and papers and cigarettes, on our dressing table are our eats for the evening: a loaf, butter, a Christmas cake and a tin of mushroom soup. Joyce has been lying on the floor battling for sound on our wireless, which is proving even less useful than our bloody little fire.

We had a church parade today, fortunately in the smaller and considerably warmer hangar with a very enthusiastic parson who urged us to be pieces of rock between interludes of calling us miserable sinners. I regrettably had a long-distance flirtation with the trumpet player. On my return I was then chivvied by the sergeant to (a) walk straight and (b) swing my arms. The first I find impossible, the second objectionable and concentrating on achieving both spoilt the dreams I have to make marching endurable. One of the warrant officers passed a lovely remark on our return to the orderly room: 'Now that you've finished your God bothering.'

13 January 1940

Coming home on leave last night I bought *Reader's Digest* and found in it this perfect thing. It's supposed to be a song chanted by a four-year-old boy in his bath each night and his mother had managed to copy down this fragment:

He will just do nothing at all, he will just sit there
    in the noon-day sun
And when they speak to him he will not answer
    them, because he does not care to
He will stick them with spears and put them in the
    garbage
When they tell him to eat his dinner he will laugh
    at them
And he will not take his nap because he does not
    care to, he will go away and play with the panda
And when they come to look for him he will put
    spikes in their eyes and put them in the garbage
He will not go out in the fresh air or eat his
    vegetables or make wee wee for them and he
    will grow thin as a marble
He will do nothing at all, he will just sit there in
    the noonday sun.

I went over to Lensbury to have lunch with Barbara[15] today (dear, kind, generous, delightful Shell, they paid all

---

[15] Barbara Cunningham – a friend from Shell.

their staff, us serving members as well, a 10 per cent increase on their salary to cover the now increased cost of living and many weeks' back increase as well).

17 January 1940

Days go on and on and nothing important happens in them and then on a day like this it positively crams itself with incredible happenings. Little things first, equipment starts to arrive, first batches of uniforms after we have waited so long with promises of enough and coats for all by Friday, because WAAFs have frozen these last few days in the snow.

The second excitement was my having a preliminary interview with a view to a code and cipher commission, which I don't think I'll be given because they consider me too young.

I am sorry the description of the day's doings had been such an anticlimax but to be honest with you it's now many days later, I having been interrupted in the writing of it by a caller and then forgetting it and life being what it is the excitement is now ended.

Anyway it's now 21 January. I have been out every evening since last Tuesday and consequently feel somewhat jaded. We (Joyce and I) have drawn up the beds and are leaning against them almost in a super colossal fire. We have borrowed (with permission) the wireless from Ray and Peggy. The food is on the washstand and we are waiting for two visitors to call on us. I have to clean my buttons, which is rather a bore. I am very dirty because it's too cold to wash but I don't care. I haven't made my bed for days because I have discovered that if I crawl out carefully it will still do. In short, the layers of ladylike-hood are peeling off pretty speedily and doubtless soon I shall smell. Oh well, what the hell.

29 January 1940

What a weekend! It began on Friday when Eric was taking me to the *Little Review* with a sore throat and that aching prelude to flu plus a depression caused by Joyce's Monday departure to a very good Air Ministry job, fortunately quite near Hendon. Feeling frightful and having to meet Eric, I stumbled into a chemist from the rain and blackout and demanded that he gave me something to pep me up for the night. Dubiously and unwillingly he gave me a bright brown scalding liquid like fifteen fiery cocktails combined (I do love alliteration), which not only put me on top form for the whole evening but has kept me there ever since. I enjoyed myself very much, we ate and danced and laughed loudly at the *Little Review*, which was slick and modern, clever and Oh! The genius of Hermione Baddeley as an ancient prima suprima, colisima ballerina, or the most Novelloist of Novello gipsy heroines! Afterwards we had a taxi back to Waterloo in which he was so good that I am afraid he may be wanting to be serious and he saw me off to Claygate asking if I'd see the *Gate Review* with him on his next leave. He's a very nice boy, I don't want him to be hurt, but I've no feeling about him at all.

On Saturday evening I met Joyce in town and we went over with some friends of hers to a dance at her old home in Blackheath. It was quite good fun but I would have enjoyed it more had my voice not been so faint but speaking seemed too great an effort to bother over much.

I was supposed to return to Hendon last night but owing to the snow there weren't any trains. I had hell's delight getting back here (Claygate) on Sunday morning as every electric train had gently died on the nation. I eventually got a steam train as far as Surbiton (passing en route a notice flaunting the words 'And still the railways carry on'). This morning there is still no train so I am back again by the welcome home fire warming up for a second attempt after lunch starting with a cab to Surbiton.

1 February 1940

I have been moved out of house number 18 to number 11 and have been put in temporary charge of it until the return of a very nice corporal friend of mine, René Le Mesurier. Its other inhabitants are old and staid and utterly law abiding with a conscience over helping with the housework. I am none of these, with a livid reputation for breakfast lateness. It's half past ten now, I'm on a pouffe before a very hot fire and a half-read American *Ladies Home Journal*.

8 February 1940

For weeks I've wantonly escaped it, tonight there was no further eluding it. I am on duty on the telephone. That unpleasantness means that you sit from five to nine in the WAAF Recreation Room, if you're like me with both feet in the fire, and when the phone rings you have to answer it and, depending on your conscience, say either 'leave a message' or 'I'll see if I can find her'.

On the wireless a frightful band of men are singing over and over again the same song interspersed with remarks of dullness about keeping on key and top Bs by another man with a shaking voice. I've got to keep it on, it's my only means of knowing six o'clock. I've got cigarettes, my knitting, this diary and a magazine. I can't sincerely be martyred, especially if I did want to go out, I've got no money and owe odd WAAFs 11/6d.

Up and down Booth Road WAAFs are cleaning windows, hiding beer bottles and Dillon is reluctantly black-leading a grate. Big bugs from Air Ministry are coming tomorrow to billet inspect. My room will be the only one not with its morning face. The orderly sergeant has now arrived and is battling with the intricacies of the NAAFI finances. I've combined three good deeds tonight but I've resigned the struggle. I've helped the cooks wash up and I'm taking someone's place in the decontamination squad so that she can leave camp. I glow with a large pro-social feeling.

28 February 1940

Two weeks' interlude between this and the last entry represents a week in the WAAF sickbay with a cold and pink eye and five days in an isolation hospital with measles, separated by two delightful days of sick leave seeing both the *Gate Review* and *Funny Side Up* with Eric. I was talking while in sickbay with a girl about platonic friendship, the way you do get talking very late in the night with neither of you tired through too much bed, and she said it never worked because the very fact that you were men and women made one of you at some point, if only very briefly, have feelings for the other. That's true. Sitting beside Eric in *Funny Side Up*, he in his new undress uniform and I in the unaccustomed femininity of a pretty frock, this dialogue just over between us:

Joan: 'Mind you've caught my frock.'

Eric: 'Joan, you're getting me in quite a state.'

Joan: 'Is that the effect the frock has on you?'

Eric: 'The frock or you.'

I got the first feeling I had for him of sentimentality but now it's gone and I feel nothing again.

I read somewhere else that a woman who can inspire love and not even feel pity is a dangerous and unhappy character.

8 March 1940

I am becoming a most domesticated girl. The mornings see me sweeping, dusting and bed making and even cleaning the windows of my room, and most surprising, liking it. Housework, I see, is nothing like as soul destroying as typing. Lunch hour saw me in shirtsleeves and mackintosh apron standing before a sink, singing tunelessly the twiddly-pom bit of 'Eighteenth-Century Minuet' and faced with piles and piles and more piles of WAAF washing up. Washing up after meals now being compulsory, one of the vast growing number of unpleasantnesses that are compulsory these days. I can't say I enjoyed that but thought hard of soldiers being killed for England and me only being inconvenienced, which helped me along.

Yesterday evening I decided not to go to the station dance as I had a cold, so put on slacks, many jerseys, mittens and a scarf and went out into the back garden where I weeded and dug and generally prepared the earth for its invasion of seeds on Sunday and finished off with a truly colossal bonfire which brought all the little boys from far and wide to watch the fun. Digging there in the mildness of an early spring evening, with the faint sound of other WAAF voices on the billet the other side and a few children climbing in and out of air raid shelters, left me at peace. I had no thoughts beyond the moment; all emotion had run out of the world; it was only the pleasant day and the earth heavy under my fork and my own satisfied tiredness. All this is probably just my

34

way of saying there's something in this gardening racket after all.

After, I came in to find Mickey roasting before my fire and we drank her soup, toasted my bread and ate my mother's marmalade. This morning I got an invitation to Barbara's wedding on 27th of this month and Our Annie, the hearty CO who has taken over from Mrs Rowley, has given me the afternoon off to go to it.

9 March 1940

This evening is Saturday. I had money and decided to go in to Hendon after tea. I walked round Woolworths, shed some several shillings and returned to Booth Road with arms containing bulbs in a pot, six packets of seeds, a face flannel, a tin of boot polish, a duster, a vase, flowers, needles and cotton, a garden trowel and a packet of soap flakes. Back in my room I've lit my fire, cleaned three pairs of shoes, washed several stockings and am preparing for a snug evening before a now burning fire mending clothes and listening to the wireless, supplemented by toast and Stork[16] and marmalade and climaxed by a bath.

Yesterday evening Mickey and I and other deluded WAAFs went through the blackout and into the wilds of Hammersmith enduring the journey with the thought of the rollicking, witty West End show, *Broadway Follies*,

---

[16] Stork margarine.

studded with stars, to which we WAAFs had been invited free. I might say frightful, I might say terrible, awful, boring, tedious, but they only reveal the inadequacy of words. After the third hour, or so it seemed, I was convinced that I had died and was in hell, watching turn after turn in unending procession, each longer, each less funny, each more unbelievably bad than the last. During the interval, Hendon WAAFs rushed to the bar, scruffy WAAFS, obviously from West Drayton, sat still rollicking with mirth in the Stalls. We tossed back whisky and ginger beer and watched in a stupor the longer, duller, apparently unending second half. After came the journey back in the blackout made blue by our opinions of the evening.

11 March 1940

How nice it is to listen in the mornings to the BBC broadcasting physical jerks[17] when one has no intention whatsoever of doing them. Our Annie and I have practically no point of common interest. She's a large strapping woman with appalling legs and heaps of hearty laughter. Her spiritual home is in a damp tent with a smoking campfire and a brood of nasty little Girl Guides. In fact, I believe between being a general's daughter she was once a Girl Guide captain.

I went with Mickey and Frances to the pictures tonight

---

[17] A morning exercise programme on the radio.

and came back arguing about politics and the future of England. Obviously England is a declining power; obviously Communism has come to stay; obviously the breaking of British class barriers is a long overdue necessity if the country's ever to survive. Do you realise only 3 per cent of our populace, the lucky percentage with a public school education, can ever hope to receive any of the really first-rate jobs? Oh, the colossal conceit of a country, to limit its selection of brain ability from a future 3 per cent. There is so much wrong with the world, so much in a nightmarish muddle. Still there is this consolation: it's a bad world but it's not a dull one. It's got evil and stupidity and muddle but it's also got excitement and adventure and variety. For the cynical, for the without illusions, one can still live zestfully and not yearn too unbearably for Utopia.

15 March 1940

I am home and tired, I've been out every night this week. Tomorrow morning I shall lie in a soft warm bed and stretch out a languid hand to my bell, which will bring my breakfast to me. Tonight I shall dissolve the grime of ages (three days and nights) in a large boiling bath.

I've got to give up my room. The corporal whose rightful residence it is has decided she wants it and I am to have the front double room, so very much more to clean. I am sick and sorry; I like my room. I like the sixpenny and flourishing plant on the windowsill. I like the string from the light via the door to my bed which enables me to extinguish both light and wireless without getting back into the cold. I like it because it is little and easy to warm and has clean windows and a polished floor. I wish I were a corporal and not so tired. I am writing this all odd: it was going to be very artful introducing all the week's events in so natural a manner that one slipped easily into the other.

Allow me, says she in her best pompous author manner, to take you from my usual haunts of Booth Road and Claygate and that part of London encircling Leicester Square into the hitherto unexplored region of Hendon Aerodrome. If we are lucky, as we enter its gates, the police on duty will salute me and make me feel very smooth. Why then, reader, do I hurry? Why have I paid unusual trouble with my toilet and clutch in my hand a limp paper when usually I saunter past late, untidy and sucking a Zube? I am going to a Messing meeting as a representative of WAAF airwomen, that's why – a role strangely thrust on me by Our Annie.

We gather in the messing officer's room, the WAAFs waved politely to chairs, the airmen soldiers standing self-consciously behind us. After a pause, which I passed looking out of the window unaware that I was expected to speak and thinking how rude it was that nobody did so, I, as WAAF representative, am asked to complain first. I blushed a lot and said the WAAFs wanted more fruit.

That noted, Pilot Officer Burton turned to the men and the fun began. They said their fried bread was hard. The sergeants, two harsh-faced individuals, said it was inevitable on account of the ovens; Pilot Officer Burton strove courageously to pacify both parties. Throughout the battle, which travelled through hard fried bread to bread at dinner to too thin tea, he remained courteous, fair and eternally anxious to help the men. This was definitely one of the better Service customs. The men get direct to the officers with their complaints.

As a result of this morning meeting, far from finishing my work at the customary 4.15, when I left at 4.45 it was yet undone. At 5 p.m. when I was preparing to go to town, a trembling WAAF informed me that an angry Annie was on the phone demanding my return to finish my work. I returned swearing all up Booth Road and by the time I got to her my anger had surprisingly gone. I accepted, not very well concealing my smiling lack of penitence, her and Henderson's bawling, so that at the end they were smiling too. I like Henderson, she is small and attractive and tough.

20 March 1940

WAAF whisklets –

Mr Dunne, giving Frances Baxter a packet of Smarties: 'You've got a habit I don't like.'

Frances: 'What's that?'

Mr Dunne: 'You breathe.'

Mr Dunne is a civilian clerk under whose care we WAAFs at Station Headquarters are. He has promised to lift me one of those 'You never know who's listening' posters for my billet.

Mickey Johnston has a driving test. 'Don't let her drive inside the aerodrome,' warns a sergeant to the girl who accompanies her on her test, suspecting Mickey's ability with tragic truth. From the WAAF Mess to the aerodrome gates Mickey takes the wheel. She flashes down Booth Road, her companion beginning to be uneasy and success and speed intoxicating her, and as she takes the corner sends two milk cans hurtling down the road. She misses a swearing stag-like leaping wing commander by inches and jams on the brakes to a halt in front of the frozen face of a station policeman. Mickey has not driven for some years and then only in Prague and on the wrong side of the road. The nearly run-over wing commander was very, very mad. Only much effort, not helped by Mickey's merry laughter as she sat in the van, destruction right and left, got her out of being put on a charge.

21 March 1940

In the afternoon Frances and Evans, with the solemn, nervously smiling faces of people who know their expressions ought to be sad, came to say, 'We came to tell you something dreadful has happened. Oliver's husband has been killed.' Oliver used to work with me; she's only been married six weeks; her husband was one of the Hendon sergeant pilots. He crashed near Birmingham and the plane caught fire.

Later, I went into our officers' room and reminded Annie that I was having Wednesday off for Barbara's wedding, and Mrs Burley, the Code and Cipher Officer, said she too was going to a wedding on Wednesday. I said it couldn't be the same one and she said 'Howroyd', and I said 'David', and the whole room shrieked because it is the same one.

After tea: sitting in the Recreation Room on guardroom duty, hearing more details about Oliver's husband, and everybody telling other dreadful accidents.

24 March 1940

Yesterday evening Bridget, Boompsie and I went to a dance at the Overseas Club to meet Canadians. Before I went I knew I was going to enjoy it, despite spots on my face through overeating and not being energetic enough. I had one of my moods when nothing mattered. Anyway the spots were only few and small and make-up covered them.

When we got there a Paul Jones[18] was in progress and the end of it found me with an officer: very Canadian, very tight and a very good dancer. While others danced decorously around, we trucked and shagged and said 'ha cha cha', all his instructions to me being prefaced with a 'honey child'. I felt like the whole of *Gone With the Wind*. By the time the next Paul Jones was over I was somewhat weary and ended that with a young French Canadian soldier who took me to supper and with whom I spent the rest of the evening. He's twenty-two and his

---

[18] Popular dance in which partners change regularly.

name is Gerry. He's not good looking nor very well bred but he's young and fresh and I liked him a lot. I enjoyed it all.

At the end both of us wanted to make a date. I was only able to tell him my address and as he's new to London and doesn't speak much English I doubt if it registered; pity because he was fun.

This morning I was woken by Bridget at 7.30, said 'what the hell' and went to sleep till 9.30, when I had to tear to work without any breakfast. I had meant to have a quiet afternoon reading and gardening and having a necessary bath, but Eric phoned up and said he was free till seven o'clock, so I went up to town and we went to the zoo. He asked me out next Friday. I only have a French class, which I could have postponed, but I heard myself refusing. I cannot accept every time he asks me.

That beastly sergeant who wouldn't give the men soft fried bread has been put on a charge for swiping coal; I'm very glad.

28 March 1940

This new diary is much too small but it is all that the shop had. I'm starting it off anyway in proper style with a description of Barbie's wedding. Yesterday, a quarter to two saw me waiting for a bus outside Simpson's in Piccadilly. I was looking very smart and clean with my hair newly set, my buttons shining and I was wearing my Moss Bros best blue.

This part of London was sleek and prosperous with

its offices and 'not-having-to-think-about-having-to-take-a-taxi' people. The sun was shining on its large solid buildings.

In the church I sat by Beasle, a girl from Shell, and I was hardly seated when the congregation rose and in came the bride. I suppose all brides are beautiful but it was hard to believe that for the last two years I had worked and played and talked and eaten with so wonderful looking a person. I couldn't see them at the altar very well, nor hear David's replies, but Barbara's voice was steady and distinct. Then they went up to the altar and knelt down by it together. I saw them hold each other's hands and I said over and over and over in my head, don't kill David. There was a pause, silent and excited and expectant, when they came out of the vestry and then the organ burst out 'Here Comes the Bride' and they came past us, smiling and married.

I was a bit wary about the reception. The one wedding I'd been to before had a reception that I hated: I'd not known anyone and I was lost and embarrassed and shy. I was grateful and glad therefore when all Barbara's relatives I had met at her twenty-first birthday party came and welcomed me with at least an externally perfect sincerity. After a series of champagnes I began to love everyone present. My shyness melted and giggles replaced it. Peter and another boy and girl and I grouped in a corner and collected all the available champagne and got to that lovely floating stage where everything was very very funny. Occasionally I detached myself and chatted animatedly to total strangers, but I always came back to Peter, the Cunninghams' very nice cousin, and Biddy and Patsy, Barbara's almost-as-nice-as-her sisters.

After my fourth champagne there was one moment when I felt worried because things really were getting rather odd and words slipped about in my mouth. However, I rallied all my will-power and kept Biddy by me, who has a head like a rock even if only fifteen. She and Barbara are very alike, while Patsy and I are the silly ones. Then I formally adopted all the Cunninghams, arranged with them and Peter to go down for a weekend and was led by Biddy to my hat and gas mask. By great concentration I got to Mother's office to tell her that the bride carried a lovely wreath of spring flowers.[19]

1 April 1940

Coming back here in the Tube last night I thought, 'This can't be real, I'm dreaming a nightmare, people can't be as ugly as that row opposite me.' They had faces like drag-coloured plasticine pulled by grubby fingers into grotesque imitations of human faces. I could hardly bear looking at their ugliness. Then other people came in and made it more endurable: a young soldier with a face like a cheerful Walt Disney dwarf, a red-cheeked baby with a head circled with small ginger curls and a woman with a pale face, hollow cheeks and a long lovely mouth.

On Saturday at home it was sunny and I walked over

---

[19] My parents ran their own wholesale gown business called 'Bawden's Gowns'.

to Esher to change my library book. Weekends are almost the only time I get for reading now. In the weekdays I'm busy living. Books show you so much though. This weekend I had a good haul: *A Life of Christ*, Lewis Golding's *The Jewish Problem* and seven plays of 1939, including an excellent one by Lillian Hellman, *The Little Foxes*, and Terence Rattigan's very thin and very empty *After the Dance*.

Eric has a week's leave this week. I am seeing Walt Disney's *Pinocchio* and two plays with him. He suggested that we went to see *Cousin Muriel*: I don't think he likes serious plays very much but he thinks I do.

4 April 1940

Last night Eric and I went to see Cochran's (I thought disappointing) *Lights Up*. I'm beginning to be very fond of Eric. The trouble with youth is we are brought up to believe in and expect a Romeo and Juliet romance and that comes so rarely. If we were taught to expect nothing romantic from life, if we were only taught to see life intelligently, clear of literature's ideas of love, if we could only have adult contact with the other sex, we would be saved so much disillusion. If only we didn't want eternal love. My only hope is that by the time I get to be thirty I may have gotten rid of moonlight and roses and can enjoy living as a sophisticated, sane, unsentimental adult.

We had a taxi from Queens Bar to the Savoy and put our feet up on the tip-up seats opposite. Mine wouldn't quite reach.

He said, 'Put yours on mine.'

'They'll make your trousers dusty.'

'It doesn't matter.'

He held both my hands.

'Curse you.'

'Why?'

'For being you.'

'I can't help it.'

I was stirred and roused so much so that I was unsatisfied and restless for some time after. I wondered what kissing with him would be like.

6 April 1940

Yesterday was one of those unpremeditated evenings that turn out fun. Frances, Mickey and I arranged to go to the pictures and half past five saw Mickey and me ready to go, pacing the pavement impatiently outside the Sergeants Mess, within which sat Frances and company sergeants chatting socially with Our Annie. Beside us in the road was Old Mort (an elderly shapeless WAAF), sitting in the hearse, which is what we have named her utility van, a horrible monster of wood and glass. However, we were not too proud to climb into it and get a lift to Colindale Station once Frances had eventually broken loose.

We found the Classic Cinema and for sixpence had the choice of any seat in the Stalls and two excellent films, one of which being *The Wandering Jew*. Frances and Mickey ate sherbets and chocolate cushions. I had toothache and just sighed sadly when they passed the bag to each other over me. We approve very much of this cinema: as Mickey said, you even get to go to the lavatory free.

That evening we fumbled through blackout and strange streets in search of a bus stop, then we smelt it – definitely, unmistakably – fried fish and chips! We went methodically down the street smelling each shop, sometimes the aroma was strong, sometimes faint, but the source always eluded us. Finally, defeated and sorrowful, we reached the bus stop. Just as the bus approached I glanced behind me one last time and there was what we wanted. I ripped the other two from the bus, we rushed inside, purchased chips and one piece of fish for Frances, and ate them while wandering lost round Hendon.

When I got back, Beck and Bridget were in the kitchen. We talked about life and love and religion and men and survival of the individual until suddenly it was half past twelve.

10 April 1940

In the event of an air raid WAAF personnel rush to the new steel and reinforced concrete shelters, excepting the Decontamination Squad who huddle in one of the already shaken Booth Road houses.

I have got myself onto the reserve of the Decontamination Squad, a first step to removing myself from it entirely. Three parts of this is ordinary cowardice, the other quarter is my rigid determination to survive and outlast this war. With the Scandinavian invasion, the war is jolted back on us, just as we had almost forgotten it.[20] We heard the wireless reports in the Recreation Room after lunch where we usually huddle over the fire, eating Milky Ways, smoking and reading the daily papers provided free for us by the RAF.

I have had to surrender my little room at last. Last night while I was at French class (for the first time I found myself speaking it fluently without hesitation and effort), the others in the house moved my belongings downstairs into the big room with two disadvantages: no privacy and more cleaning. I think and hope they felt a little guilty about it because they lit my fire and made my bed and offered to help me clean up this morning. However, provided I can keep the room from a strange WAAF invasion and get myself some curtains, cushions and carpets, I can make it reasonably comfortable.

13 April 1940

In the morning of Thursday the officer I work for snatched my *Daily Express* from my hand and said, 'Hoorah, hoorah! The war will be over in six months. The Germans have done the very worst thing now' – and a lot more hoorahs. In my heart I don't myself believe it but I spent the morning saying 'six months of war and

[20] On 9 April, Nazi forces attacked Denmark and Norway, effectively ending 'the phoney war' – the name adopted by Western Europe to reflect the lack of action since Germany had invaded Poland in September 1939.

three months of cleaning up and I'll be in Paris by next April'.

In the afternoon we went to be inoculated and filed one by one into rugged grandeur's (the doctor's) office, to have our right arms pierced by the tetanus and our left by the anti-typhoid. I had no time to wait and think about it. Everyone else was genuinely indifferent. I didn't look at the needle. I was really quite brave – an improvement anyway on my screaming days at the dentist doorstep. 'You'll feel awful in the evening,' previously inoculated WAAFs told me, 'freezing cold and nothing you can do will make you warmer.'

Accordingly, that evening I built up a colossal fire in my billet, piled blankets high on my bed with a further reserve on a chair, put on several jumpers and got to bed with a hot-water bottle, two aspirins, a box of cheeses, some broken chocolates, four buns and grapes from South Africa given to me by Bridget Prouse. I got extremely hot and soon went to sleep but the great frost came not at all. In the morning, noble to the last, I got up for breakfast. After breakfast I felt very odd and went back to bed. Finally I felt so foul I cast aside my book and unwisely toyed with the remains of last night's food. At lunchtime friends brought me a letter from Barbara. Cheered by that (she's asked me to Wales for my holidays), I tottered, pale and aching, to the Mess to work and on to a Chinese restaurant with Joyce, Mickey and Boompsie and finally feeling better to Bunty's where she and I laughed a lot about old days at school, while Mrs Goldie knitted (until she broke her needle and pulled it all undone) a year-old coat for a yet unborn baby. Eric listened and fed us with chocolates he'd brought over with him for us.

16 April 1940

On Monday Boompsie and I, having no money (Boompsie is sharing my room as it is too large for one), lit the fire, turned on the wireless, got out books, mending etc. and looked sadly at two oranges, two pieces of chocolate cake and three tired tomato-flavoured cheeses. Suddenly there was a knock at the door which I, doing a French exercise and cursing, answered. And there stood Joyce with a car and £1. I pulled on my coat over my tattered slacks (my decent pair have been being cleaned for the last three weeks and I am too poor to reclaim them), my blue shirt and my yellow jacket and we drove down to the local fish and chip shop before returning to the fireside with fish and chips and lemonade and ginger beer. Joyce stayed till 11.30 and we laughed practically continuously.

Yesterday after meeting Mother I went on to my French class where Professor Bolitho told me of his love affairs, beginning at the age of eleven and apparently yet unended, with the seduction of a Girl Guide captain as the highlight. I enjoyed hearing it. I enjoyed discussing the varying moral outlooks of English and Europeans. I enjoyed his constant praise of me with remarks such as '*J'aime les jeunes filles robustes fortes comme vous*'. It did me good but after I left him my exit was shattered by the fact that I tripped and sprawled down the first flight of his stairs.

Going from there, I hurried through the rain to Lyons Corner House to meet dear old Margot Ainscough from Shell, in the uniform of an ATS.[21] We went from there to the Regent Palace Bar where we discussed the varying lives of WAAF and ATS greatly to the Air Force's favour – so much so, in fact, that she's going to see if she can't get a transfer to the WAAF.

Before I forget, snappy Service sayings: 'Up with the lark and to bed with the Wrens'; RAF = 'running after fluff'.

22 April 1940

Sitting in the adjutant's office and looking out of the window to where the sun was shining and aeroplanes landing on the green new grass I thought suddenly, my life is contented now: I have an interesting new job (I'm working for the new Station Intelligence Officer who's from Yorkshire and stocky and going bald, with a lot of humour and at the moment a bad cold. He treats you as if you had as much intelligence as himself); I have a reasonably nice young man, Eric, and enough variety to keep away boredom from my leisure hours. Never in my life have my days been so round and snug and this is a war, a clash of civilisation. It is odd.

[21] Army Territorial Service, which recruited women to work in the Army.

25 April 1940

Last night the WAAFs gave a dance. I had my hair done the night before and it was looking extremely nice. Everyone had been remarking on it, the boys in the Orderly Room teasing me about it. Just before I left the house, Boompsie called from the bathroom to say the tap had burst again, but as Becket, the house NCO, said she would get a plumber, I thought no more about it.

I danced with a lot of airmen, none very exciting, and at about 11.30 I met Boompsie and a drunk young Army officer: they said they were going on to a beer party when the dance ended and would I come. I said all right and we all of us went round looking for beer to buy and take away. Then one of the WAAF sergeants said she had heard about our planning and was coming along to our house to see we were in bed. I went to tell Geoffrey, the Army officer, this and explain it would be stupid to go. He said all right, come out with me tomorrow night, and kissed me in the hall in front of our senior sergeant; we were very drunk. He took my telephone number and said he'd phone. Apparently he had made likewise promises to Boompsie and others (there's a dance up at his place and he was sent to collect a few WAAFs to go, preferably, I think, of the prostitute tendency).

Back in my billet no plumber had come, the kitchen was flooded, Becket had missed the dance and spent the evening bailing water and was very very mad. Lots of men with mud-encrusted boots had worn paths across our bedroom. I got into bed with two aspirins, lied to the disappearing sergeant about Boompsie and was awakened by her at 3.30 returning from the Army officer and a battle for her maidenhead. I swore at her with a language I never realised I knew, and woke again at seven to see water over our floor, the pipes having burst in the night. Becket and I spent the morning cleaning it up, a filthy job, and by 11.30 when we were finally finished we lay like two limp dirty dolls on our respective beds.

28 April 1940

On Friday I went with Eric to see *Gone With the Wind*, having food first at the Queens Bar where we laughed and he teased and was rude to me: a far pleasanter state of affairs. The film was a good copy of the book: I know the book so well I could tell every line of every dialogue. The best parts were Scarlett returning to her ruined Tara against utmost odds – misery, poverty, starvation – and her rigid will to succeed, to rebuild. I lost interest in the beautiful silk-wrapped well-fed woman at the end of the film, beyond a sense of stupid waste as she progressed unhindered in her killing of Rhett's love. Coming out we had supper and going down to my train, Eric kissed me: he didn't interest me at all.

7 May 1940

I went reluctantly with three other WAAFs and a lot of airmen in a large coal lorry over to Uxbridge to go to the dentist. The Air Force is really wonderful: even dental treatment is given us free. It's a comforting feeling to be fed and clothed and kept healthy by an impersonal higher being – it leaves so little to worry about. No wonder the Services are happy go lucky.

I have never been to such a good dentist who took endless trouble and never once hurt me. I had three injections for stopping the pain and have to go tomorrow to have one out.

The journey back was fun: it was a hot day so we rolled up the battered tarpaulin and the wind caught in it like a sail almost lifting us from the road. The airmen laughed and talked and the van rattled us about and everyone in the street stopped to smile at us. In the evening I cut the grass and cleaned the window – it's house inspection tomorrow.

9 May 1940

I began to be afraid in the morning. I began to think he couldn't possibly take out a whole hard tooth without hurting me. By lunchtime, as I walked down to the waiting dentist lorry, past a lorry full of cheering WAAFs going to play hockey, I felt very self-sorry. This time I rode with Pat Rollandson in front with the driver.

In the waiting room I found an article on 'Why Be Afraid' and drained it of its inadequate comfort. An orderly called, 'ACW Bawden' and I walked to the chair. He stuck needles in my tooth and said, indifferently of course, that it wouldn't hurt me. I was glad he wasn't sympathetic: I was horribly unreasonably afraid. The agony was wondering when it would hurt. I said, 'I will be brave, I do so want to be brave,' and one tear fell out of the side of my eye but nobody took any notice of it. Suddenly two hands came out behind my head and held it fast, I screwed up my eyes, his pincers were on my tooth and he was right! It didn't hurt. My faith in him returned, I wondered with interest how long it would take to come out. He had to get another pair of pincers and pulled and pulled, and the orderly gripped my head and at last, without a twinge, I felt it slipping out. He made me put my head between my knees to fill the cavity with blood. I have to go back next week but I don't mind. Next time I'll be really properly brave.

That evening Boompsie and I went to Golders Green to see Ivor Novello's empty, faintly amusing *Full House*. I am writing this later, bored and on guardroom duty. Hearty Annie has just come in to say goodbye to us, I wonder what officer horror they've found for us next.

It's even later now and I'm back in my billet from the Sergeants Mess. They'd had a party and had a lot of food left over, so Priscilla Carpenter and I were asked in to eat it up (my appetite is famous) and it was heavenly – gherkins and cheese and crisps and prawns and olives and beer, yummy yum.

11 May 1940

These last two days!

Boompsie's wake-up call: 'Joan!', and Broadcast

Control's: 'Collect no. 5 equipment',[22] woke me at dawn. Stumbled cursing from bed to gather armfuls of warm clothes and paid a thoughtful visit to the Auntie[23] (sanitary arrangements in our air raid shelters are supported by two inadequate and immodest buckets).

Returned to bed to hear much-welcomed 'No. 5 equipment not required', instead of the expected siren, and stumbled tired to breakfast to hear Holland and Belgium had been invaded. Felt a rush of joy that the fighting has been worthwhile. England may be imperfect but at least we try to do right; at least we never started this war; at least we never invaded and bombed neutral countries.

Cleaned the billets after breakfast to hear a clatter and breaking glass and rushed to the window in time to see the local dairy horse rushing down the road and the cart and milkman sprawling in the road.

Went to SHQ[24] to hear that all leave was indefinitely cancelled and felt at last that I was no longer a civilian an employee of Shell but a member of the Air Force.

Played tennis, lay in the sun reading, and felt bitter and resentful at the selfishness and hypocrisy of America. Just let them, at the end of the war, come smug and self-satisfied and try to tell us who has fought and how to dictate our peace. America, seat of democracy, something's rotten in that state of Denmark. If they stay out of Europe's war they can stay out of her peace.

[22] Gas mask and decontamination kit.
[23] Lavatory.
[24] Station Headquarters.

Working hard at SHQ and saw this afternoon the biggest force so far of the war: three Belgian planes of the Sabina Airline landing at Hendon.

15 May 1940

This morning, through the surrender of Holland's news, I went on my last visit to the dentist. The journey over was dull, the airmen were decorous and polite. We three WAAFs sat silent and unsmiling together. My dentist is sweet and small and solemn and not much smiling, with one of those sorts of humour that amuses him more than outside people. When I went in he was swinging himself round on a stool like a comic Puck.

18 May 1940

It began to be like a war yesterday night, we slept badly disturbed almost hourly by 'Orders to Pilot' by Broadcast Control. At 6.30 Joyce woke us by knocking at the door; she'd been up since 4 a.m. driving.

All day I worked hard and outside my windows planes came and went: Ensigns, Hurricanes, Lockheeds, Spitfires and the beautiful Belgian planes of the Sabina Airline.[25] Belgian pilots from the Sabina Airline who had escaped from Belgium have come here these last three days into intelligence sections for passes. My newly

[25] Bringing anyone they could find back from France.

polished French has been proudly and usefully exploited.

In the evening Margaret Jennings and I went up to town to Joyce's twenty-first cocktail party and met the most fascinating squadron leader who knew every bit how attractive he was to women. I envied his poise, his assurance, his confidence, his impenetrable self-belonging and untouchedness.

Today I have been hearing about the state of events in Belgium and Holland: fear-mad men and women on a refugee ship bombed and machine-gunned by Nazi planes and having to be shot by the ship's sailors, terror having made them beyond any control; the tattered orderless ribbons of the butchered Dutch Army; the unbelievable horror of man's inhumanity to man.

19 May 1940

Yesterday, after I had written this up, I lay in the garden and read and dozed and ate chips and chocolate and biscuits. At seven o'clock Boompsie said, 'Let's go and play tennis.'

Molly Riley was waiting for us and for about an hour we played, plied at the interval with shandy by Warrant Officer Knight.

Coming away we saw two of the Belgian pilots, one of whom had been in to the office to get a permit from me, so I said, '*Bonsoir, monsieur, qu'est ce que vous faites?*' and we talked to them for some ten minutes, I translating for Boompsie and Molly with their few words of limited French. Then Warrant Officer Knight called

'Why don't you come inside all of you?' from the Sergeants Mess so we and the Belgians did, joined by a third Belgian, a captain who not only looked like Charles Boyer but had his charm.

We had a great fun evening, drinking and talking a mixture of bad French and stumbling English and laughing a lot. Walking back with us, Captain Chartier sang softly 'J'attendrais'. None of us this morning can look at English men.

This morning Hargreaves[26] came in with his hair blown about and looking happy and said that he was hungry. He had been flying that morning, plotting out possible points where German parachutists could land. This afternoon he's gone off in a car to check up on them, so I'm here in the billet just out of a bath and in shorts, preparing to go back in the garden and sprawl in the sun.

22 May 1940

At a quarter to eight I said to Boompsie and Becky, who were dancing on Blake's polished and prized floor to 'J'attendrais', 'Let's go out and get a drink.' We went to the Hendon Way and I drank my first whisky and liked it. We ate ham sandwiches and chips, and the man at the piano played the tunes we asked for. Then a woman came over, a little, nervous, unhappy woman and said might she buy us a coffee. Her son was in the Air Force. He

[26] The Intelligence Officer I worked for.

was in France and she hadn't heard from him for a fortnight. We thanked her and she and her husband joined our party. They bought us two more whiskies and he danced with us, each in turn. We toasted Pat, her son, who's twenty-two. We've heard about the shambles in France and the bombing and machine-gunning of our squadrons there and were afraid in our hearts that her Pat was dead. But we told her encouragingly that no news was good news. Her hand shook as she drank her whisky and her cigarette dropped three times on the floor. We arranged to meet them at the Hunters Horn at Mill Hill on Saturday.

When they had gone three Air Force officers came in. Boompsie knew one of them and they asked us to join them. We had two more rounds of drinks; this time I had grapefruit. We laughed a lot and said silly empty sentences, then we all went home, parting smiling at the top of Booth Road.

This morning, after an interrupted night through an air raid warning, I leant in the empty Intelligence Office, watching the rain outside and the back of my head feeling it had been hit there, and the news said the Germans had reached Calais.

3 May 1940

They had a Sergeants Dance last Friday. Boompsie and I went in to Hendon to get our hair done for it. I was tired and irritable and my nerves were on edge. I was beginning to feel it, this not having any leave.

After, because we had just been paid and were rich, we went to eat frankfurter sausages without the sauerkraut because of the war, and cakes and coffee at a continental café. A hidden gramophone played 'Buffalo Girl Come Out Tonight' and extracts from *Carmen*. The proprietress, a thin, middle-aged woman with her hair tied up in a bun and smoking cigarettes, came over and spoke to us about the international feeling growing in us all: how we are no longer British or French or Belgian or Dutch, but man, and about Communism and women taking a bigger part in the government of the world. It was so interesting we had to hurtle back to change in time for the dance.

At the dance there was nobody there I knew and suddenly I thought, hell, I won't have this be a dud evening. I am as attractive as anyone here, so I went up and spoke to a bunch of our new squadron officers and sergeant pilots, and said, 'Did they know if Pilot Officer Tompkins were here tonight.' We met Tompkins that night in the Hendon Way. After a little talk David, one of the officers, and I danced and kind chance produced Tompkins also on the dance floor so that made talking to them appear less blatant.

From then on the evening went wonderfully, I enjoyed it most of any dance ever. The new squadron is young and gay and fun. I danced with a lot of them and joked and drank, taking care not to get drunk. I teased them about their crash (one of the pilots a day or two before had landed and forgotten to lower his undercarriage). I said it was the first ever at Hendon, so David pointed to a tall fair young sergeant pilot who had been drinking too

61

much beer and said, 'There's the culprit, you'd better tell him off.'

I spent the rest of the evening with him; his name is Don. It got hot dancing in heavy uniform so we went out and walked about. After a while we went back inside and danced again until almost the end of the dance when he took me home in his car.

In the morning I saw the sun and I laughed as if I'd been suddenly awakened, suddenly made completely alive. I was happy all day and I knew Don would phone. I met him at a quarter to eight coming towards me in his car. We saw one and a half of two very bad films and a newsreel,[27] ending with ruined Belgium and tanks breaking across the beauty of fields. I had to try hard not to cry. This is our world: war and death and dreadfulness. We are a generation without a tomorrow, alive and beautiful in our lovely today. Everybody before us has always had a tomorrow. Sayings about tomorrow such as 'you'll regret it', 'it won't work out' and 'pleasure today, pain tomorrow' have ruled their todays. But we can do whatever we please because we are without a tomorrow – and our payment for our selfish present is death.

We came out of the cinema and drove to a pub at Elstree, supposedly patronised by film stars. On the way a car with a lot of shouting passed us full of some of Don's co-sergeant pilots. We joined up at this pub and

[27] With every showing of a film at the cinema there was always ten minutes of news – Pathé News usually, opening with the cockerel crowing – which reported events around the world.

people eyed me enviously in the bar, with the four of them so young, so good looking. They make you want to describe them as they do in silly magazine stories: knights of the air, gay gallants, splendid youth. We ate eggs and chips and beer and large slices of bread in the back parlour and then they drove off in their car and Don and I in his. He has to go to Uxbridge for a three-day R/T[28] course. If he can he's going to come over in the evening, if not I shall see him Thursday when he comes back. I'm writing this in the garden, they've given me Sunday till this evening off. I needed it.

6 June 1940

The Duchess of Gloucester came yesterday to inspect WAAFs at Hendon. The whole camp was cleaned beyond recognition, we were posed in rooms we never ordinarily work in, grouping self-conscious and silly round strange desks and filing cabinets, all part of a process known as 'Preparing for an informal visit so that Her Royal Highness can see us under everyday working conditions'. She came into the Orderly Room at eleven o'clock, pathetically tiny, very pretty and becoming in her uniform and so dreadfully nervous and shy. I think she breathed hard before she came into the room, she had a the-sooner-I-do-it-the-sooner-it-will-be-over air, poor little soul. Royalty does live a dog's life. I'd like to do a skit on a royal

[28] Radio and Telephone course.

family praying for a revolution, praying to be deposed, for an ordinary normal life free from endless openings and stone layings and ceremonies and inspections and fed to the teeth with their sickening loyal populace.

9 June 1940

Life is so untidy, fiction so much better behaved. Well, if I must be honest I have to tell you truthfully about Don. It would be so much easier to pretend that I am violently, eternally in love, that at last a great passion is mine. Instead: unromantic truth. I am an inexperienced child, dabbling, a little afraid, but not wanting to step into sex with no other tie between either of us but our youth and enjoying this playing at love. In a way I'm lucky: I'm not self-deluded, then I could have believed his 'we have so little time but it's only natural and right'. I could have made my theatrical gesture of casting off convention and self-deluded myself into surrendering up my virginity. Instead a cold, bored, unsquashable voice said inside (as he swore, 'Trust me, darling, I swear it's all right') 'Don't you be a bloody fool, they all say that.' And bloody fool I wasn't. It's difficult to abandon your-self with complete bliss with this cynical voice keeping on inside you. So I kissed him and said unpersuadedly 'No' and labelled the evening positively in my brain as experience. It's not that I think virginity is so very impor-tant but self-respect is far more so and, not loving him, I would have despised myself for so long after and hating yourself is foul. You can't get away from yourself.

11 June 1940

It was theatrical and romantic, the way we heard about Italy's declaration of war. Boompsie and I went up to town to the flicks, my suspicion that it wouldn't be worth waiting in for Don's promised phone call being justified. We saw Charles Boyer in *Le Bonheur*, and Nelson Eddy in *Balalaika*. Nelson Eddy has the most beautiful voice and the music in it, if hackneyed to a little-knowing-about-music person like me, was fresh and wonderful. The 'Toreador' from *Carmen*, the 'Volga Boatmen' and then the wondrous 'Stille Nacht' sung on Christmas Day, first by the faint voices of Austrian troops in their trenches and then taken up from them by Nelson Eddy in the Russian trenches. It was so beautiful I wanted to cry.

When we came out we walked down to the Corner House to get a coffee; it was almost dark. A girl was calling out, '*Daily Worker*, *Daily Worker*, Italy declares war on the Allies.' We looked at each other – it's impossible. We asked the newspaper seller for confirmation. 'It's true,' she told us. It made living so absurd and fantastically impossible we started to laugh, then we went down into the Brasserie and, abandoning our humble plans for coffee, ordered large lagers and plates of hors d'oeuvres, and we laughed and listened to the frenzied piano pounders' rendering of the day's successes. An interesting evening!

17 June 1940

Murphy's dead. His plane crashed this morning and he and the crew were burned out. Murphy is one of the three RAF officers we had such fun with that evening in the Hendon Way. He is the one at the Sergeants Dance whom I wouldn't dance with because I wanted to stay all the time with Don.

In the morning we heard the rumour that France had packed up; we wondered about it in the groups in the Orderly Room. At lunchtime we heard the news: France is seeking terms with the enemy for an honourable peace. After, they played Elgar's First Symphony; the music's sadness deepened my own. It's the wanton senseless slaughter of all the young and of course the smugness and indifference of the English people, in the last twenty testing years. We had twenty years to make away with war and through our own fault we failed. Those who did it deserved to die, but not us young, we are waiting now to hear the six o'clock news.

21 June 1940

I've had a wonderful week. It begins with last Tuesday when Molly and I and two other WAAFs went to play tennis. Four sergeants were also wanting to play so we took turns to play sets and sat while they played, talking on the grass. The Sergeants Mess is next to the court and the WAAFs being WAAFs and sergeants being sergeants we were not long alone. While we were playing a sergeant pilot came past. He had several days of beard, flying boots, no hat and pipe and a gay grin and a very glad eye. I said to Molly, 'He looks alluring' and then forgot him and went on playing.

Next Boompsie came over from swimming and talked to a very young, very sweet little pilot called Chas. They were joined by the bearded stranger, now shaved and washed and very attractive (Johnny was his name).

In the end, still in tennis clothes, the four of us went to the Hendon Way with Chas and Johnny and two other sergeants. We had a lot of fun and it was a fooling firting evening, only I had had no tea and was very tired and the drink, which is rare these days, went to my head, so that when we went back I sat in the front of the car and went to sleep on Molly, not caring that Johnny was in the back with Boompsie and Philippa (Philippa is one of those ripe and ready girls). I woke up when the car stopped, the back clinch seemed pretty fixed so I said, 'Goodnight, I'm tired, I'm going in' and I walked across the road and did not bother about Johnny's 'Wait a minute, Joan'.

I was very surprised when, undressed and in bed, Molly (on her way to decontamination) said that Johnny wanted me to go out with him tomorrow and hadn't been able to ask me because of Philippa. I thought, 'Oh, well, I might as well, he's very attractive it will probably be fun.'

I played tennis all the next afternoon and got sunburned and got myself ready with satisfactory results for the arrival of Johnny and Chas. We went swimming first, Molly and I watched Chas and Johnny go in and I held Johnny's gun.

After, when we were drinking, Hendon phoned up recalling Chas who had to fly his plane to Doncaster that night. We drove back to Hendon, piled his clothes into the car and drove over to the plane. Then Johnny drove us to the other side of the aerodrome, parked the car in the Officers Mess, led us hatless to the forbidden stretch of runway to wave the plane goodbye, drove the car when it was gone over the group captain's taboo stretch of parade ground and was only just prevented by a swooning service policeman from driving along the group captain's own and jealously kept secret strip of private road. Johnny came back from France that morning, he doesn't care much about regulations.

Next, lamenting Chas, we went to the Hendon Way. Upstairs we had the restaurant to ourselves; we had mixed grill and white wine. Johnny was a publisher pre-war and then started the travelling library idea. He was one of the first to join the Air Force Expansion scheme in 1934 when he was twenty-eight and I think he's done lots for his years. He was in the same squadron as Cobber Kain[29] in France. After the meal we went downstairs and danced. I saw an Air Force officer sitting lonely by himself. The wine and Johnny's dancing had made me happy so I laughed at him as we went by so that when Johnny had danced with Molly he came over and asked me to dance. As a result he, Ralph, joined our party and he and Molly were both pleased to have met. At 11.30 Ralph said he

[29] Edgar 'Cobber' Kain (1918–40), the New Zealand fighter pilot who became the first Allied Ace of the war.

would drive us back and we went out somewhere in the country.

There was a high white moon and a lovely sky and Johnny began to make love. I wouldn't. I don't really know why, I just couldn't easily get roused, I had been liking him too much. It was spoiling it all, to be treated at the end of it like a tart. He was going away in the morning, so I told him my muddled thoughts. He said, 'I don't like it either, cramming weeks into hours, but it's all I've got. We none of us have time these days, everything inevitably has to be rushed. It's no good regretting, we can't alter what we have.'

He told me, 'In France we had women, it didn't mean anything, it was like turning a tap on and off. This evening can be whatever you make it, it's yours, no one can touch it. It can be as high or as low as you care. Even if I'm alive when the war ends I'll never go back to my life before, after what I've seen. This life I have to lead, I can't believe again in the things that used to be important. That is the tragedy of war: it kills some and blunts the rest of their purpose.'

I think he got tired of my shilly-shallyness and held my chin and kissed me. I've never been kissed by an adult before, it hurt and was hard and fierce and frightening. I pushed him away because I didn't like it and wanted him to do it again. He was stronger and older than I. He then said, 'I've got to go now but I'll come back.' I won't insult the evening by saying he won't. If he doesn't, I'll believe it was because he couldn't. The car stopped and we said nothing. He walked me to the gate, kissed me once gently and said, 'Au revoir, be good.' I said, 'Take care of yourself and come back soon,' so he went away out of my life.

The next afternoon I had to go to Jean Wallace's wedding. In the church I knew nobody and thought, 'This is going to be a wash-out.' Then two Army captains, one old and Irish and one younger and nice, came and sat in the pew beside me. At the Irishman's grin, the look of haughty disdain that I had been disfavouring the church with collapsed into smiles. He passed irreverent remarks throughout the ceremony.

I went with both of them to the reception. After lots of champagne, my resolution to go to bed early vanished. They, too, were just back from France; they asked me 'please to show them the town'; they teased me and I was nicely rude back and we laughed all the evening. We went to the Regent Palace, tidied up and booked seats for the Leslie Henson show *Up and Doing*.

We went for a meal to the Queens Bar where, after a Sidecar,[30] we ate salmon mayonnaise and strawberries and cream and drank lager. The show was the best review I've seen. I'm not the snob I used to be about the theatre, all I ask now is to forget and laugh. This did both beautifully for me.

They bought me chocolates and orangeade and took me after in a taxi to Leicester Square. There was no love about it and no pain and it stopped me thinking about Johnny.

---

[30] Sidecar cocktail, made up of brandy, lemon juice and Cointreau.

28 June 1940

I have to summarise the memories of a week: seven days' leave spent with Barbara and David at Abersoch, Wales, in their bungalow halfway down a cliff between the road and the sea and rock and sand. A week of lazy days browning and fresh in the sun, the first two of them clouded with Johnny-nostalgia till I took an adult hold of myself; days of getting up at noon and talking till midnight; cooking for ourselves on a primus stove. Days of no housework-doing and slacks-wearing and comfortable house untidiness. Days touched and wistful at the happiness of David[31] and Barbara, of all of us seeing a rat and Barbie driving it from the drain with Jeyes fluid and David shooting it, of David teaching me to use a revolver, of laughing at a cowboy film, of a caller with cards coming when Barbie and I were wildly unprepared with bread on the table and clothes on the chairs and all the doors to untidy cupboards flung open. Days with time to think in them and re-find peace.

The journey back was hell till Crewe: three changes, dreary people and forty minutes' wait in utter darkness at Crewe, because, as the porter laconically informed us, there was an air raid on. When the train came in I and another woman I'd spoken to (because it was 12.30 at night and strange and dark and lonely) got a compartment to ourselves. We were about to spread out when the doors

---

[31] David Hakroid was killed in a bombing raid over Germany in 1943. Barbara never remarried.

71

were opened and two men, one of them an RAF officer I had vaguely noticed at Pwllheli, asked, 'Like a little company in there?'

They came in and the RAF officer sat by me. We talked for a long while then put out the lights to sleep. But it got hotter and stuffier and sleep went away. I said after a little while, 'I don't think I can sleep after all.' 'Don't try it,' he said, and then, 'I'm going to get some air; come with me.' The carriage was full of cigarette smoke and the blackout was unbearable so I went with him. We stood in the corridor and he put both his hands either side of me on the rail.

'I suppose you think I'm an awful heel trying to kiss you?' he said.

'No I don't, they all try it.'

He laughed. 'You can't blame me for trying. You'll make me think that you've never been kissed before.'

'Not by strangers in trains at three in the morning.'

Some more like this, then he said, 'All right, let's shake on it.'

After we had shaken hands, he said, 'I admire you for that: not kissing me.' And then we began again, shaking off the grubbiness of Air Force war living and being our own selves. He said, 'I get in an awful muddle sometimes with this eat, drink and be merry business; it doesn't work out. After the war I want a farm, it's the only way to live.' In our conversation about love he said, 'Passion doesn't last; I think having the same ideas as people and knowing them all your life is the best foundation for marriage. There's a girl at home, I'm not wildly in love

72

with her but I've known her for years and we seem to agree on most things. When I want to settle down I'll probably marry her. Anyway it's not fair to marry in a war.'

Then he told me about his life, the way you talk to strangers at strange hours in strange places: both of us in the corridor and the land outside getting brighter with dawn. His name is Alec Temperley. He's twenty-three and very tall, with green eyes and a resemblance to Errol Flynn. It was 4 a.m. when we got into Euston. He carried both our cases and I took his coat. We were dirty and tousled and all-over grimy the way trains make you feel. We had a taxi to Waterloo and walked sleepily across the station until the buffet opened at five. After coffee and biscuits he shaved and I washed and then we walked again till our train went at 7.12. He was going to see an aunt in Kingston and came as far as Surbiton with me. He asked my name. I told him 'Joan Bawden'. 'I'll remember that. We met this way so strangely, maybe we'll meet again.' I said maybe. I thought fate must be pretty fed up after engineering a most unusual meeting between two congenial people to leave their next meeting limply again to fate. He said 'How do you spell it?' then he wrote down his address and said, 'Maybe I'll write some time.' More than that what could I do?

5 July 1940

His letter came. It was a charming letter, a letter anyone would be proud to receive. A letter few people would write. A letter that said the truth and never once pretended, but people don't usually end letters to girls they want to see again soon with 'let me wish you lots of luck and success in the Service and in your own life too'. It sounds so brutally quite-without-other-meaningly final, yet he needn't have written. In a day or two I shall write back, I shall have to think very hard about the letter. I could just say, 'We may not be the right ones, we probably aren't, but I think we owe it to ourselves to try a little and see. We might be missing so much.'

10 July 1940

I don't usually write this up at three in the afternoon, I'm usually working. I've been doing PT since lunch and have given myself the rest of the afternoon off. One lot will think I'm working, the other exercising, I hope. Tomorrow I'm going for my second of three Boards[32] which must be passed before I get my goal: my commission.

11 July 1940

The abrupt ending of yesterday's entry was caused by the sad fact that they hauled me back for work after all.

Well, I went for my Board this morning: they give you no indication of how you've done but I found their

[32] Interviews.

questions elementary enough and they seemed reasonably impressed with my qualifications. All I can do now is wait to hear if I've passed and then prepare myself for the Air Ministry: the last, stiffest Board. I want it all to happen quickly, I'm outgrowing Hendon. I want to go to new places with my new self, with people who have never known me. I have to go now and wash and dress again for a concert tonight at the Police College.

19 July 1940

I'm getting so bored with Hendon, I want my commission. I passed my second selection Board, I have only the third and last and hardest. I wish it were tomorrow so that I could soon be gone.

30 July 1940

Looking down the aerodrome from my office, I conclude that I am getting mentally flabby: laziness and letting myself slip were faults I always knew lay latent, waiting for encouragement in me. Little things show it, like not darning my stockings where they show and not replacing chipped nail varnish. Now, with days of almost no work, bored by being too long at Hendon and the absence of any discipline and incentive, I know I'm going to rot. If I'm not soon taken somewhere where I have to work all day I'll get purposely and irreparably blunted.

Joyce came over yesterday to comfort my stuck-in-guardroom-duty boredom. When I was released she bought fish and chips and Tizer and a box of chocolates, and we sat talking in the darkness on my bed, about sex, and as Boompsie is on leave she stayed the night with me. I hope so much we get our commissions together.

7 August 1940

At breakfast two days ago, as I was going out of the Mess, Molly said, 'Joan, sit down, I've something to tell you.' So I sat. She'd been in town the evening before and had met an RAF officer from Harwell. Hearing Harwell and remembering my rhapsodies, she'd immediately asked him, 'Do you know Pilot Officer Temperley?'

'Good old Alec?' . . . Surely, he knew him. He'd been with him the last five months, fancy Molly knowing him! . . .

And before Molly could explain that she didn't, he asked, 'Do you know his wife? Such a sweet girl.'

His wife! I remember his voice saying, 'It isn't fair, marrying in the war, I might be injured, killed. Afterwards, when I want to settle down there's a girl at home I've known all my life, I think I'll probably marry her.' I think I scaled every emotion – disbelief, incredulity, anger, more disbelief, more anger at a perfect memory spoilt and taken from me, snatched away, trampled on and then cast, ruined, back. And then I sat down on my bed and laughed. To think of my believing all he said so implicitly! It never entered my head that he would lie. After this there will be precious little any man can tell me that I'll believe again. Men are amazing. I think of the ones I've met these last months – Alec married; that Army officer in Evans's room married a week; Joyce's selfish Johnny; Don, expecting me to sleep with him and forgetting me tomorrow; Pilot Officer Pollard, married a few months ago and then finding the infatuation dead and refusing even to go home to see his wife; Sam engaged; every drinking, woman-chasing RAF officer I've ever met. Only two men I've met could I trust: David, who's Barbara's, and Eric, who's dull.

Life's really quite funny, seen as it is, not swamped in sentiment. I want to look on life like I'm looking on Sam, that sergeant pilot I met at the dance. I knew from the first he was engaged and he doesn't know I know. In brief and in triteness: forewarned is forearmed.

I'm going to have a bath now, we've been house-cleaning and I'm very, very tired. I was out on Monday with Eric and on Tuesday with Sam and woke up at 6 a.m. strangely both mornings.

14 August 1940

Before I would let myself relax on the bed with two sandwiches, a box of cheese and an illegally borrowed magazine and book, I made myself do housework. Nobody made me do it, no one would have stopped me if I had lain the whole evening on the bed reading and eating, but because my mind has already accepted the wisdom of the saying 'you get out of life what you put into it', I worked.

Tomorrow I am twenty-one. What sort of person shall

I become? That is fate still. I still struggle from the swaddle of other people's imposed ways of living. I still experiment for my own way: what are my creeds and my code for living? My creed – self-honesty, every day I see more its great importance. Life can't be built on a sham. My code of living – I don't believe in religion's mumbo jumbo of mystical heaven and life hereafter. I believe this life here is the only life I shall ever have. I believe in the value of every experience; I believe in the full whole-heartedness living of life; I believe in obeying one's own code of conduct, not because of joy in heaven, but because to be a mean person or a selfish person or an unkind person or a cruel person is an insult to one's possibilities.

16 August 1940

It looks like the war has properly started now. London had a warning yesterday evening, while Eric, my parents, some family friends and I sat sipping sherry, celebrating my twenty-first birthday at Martinez.[33] The prospect of finding a shelter on such an occasion was more than repellent so we sat on, sipping, getting glowier and mellower, till came the All Clear. It was a good birthday, despite no first post at the beginning. Second post brought a letter from Barbie, the third one from Patsy and at lunchtime I had two telegrams and a watch from my parents. At five I met Eric who took me to Mappin and

[33] A small Italian restaurant between Oxford Street and Piccadilly.

Webb and bought me a gold identity bracelet and after to Queens where we got two drinks up on the rest of the party. We went to Hatchets in the evening after Martinez for a birthday meal, then back to Claygate for the night.

The second air raid warning was the next morning, at Waterloo on my way back to Hendon, and caused me to spend a bored, tedious hour in a vast underground arch in the company of far too many people. The third is only just over and was equally boring, spent in and out and around the Hendon shelter, trying to write, trying to read, angry at so futile a waste of time. It's a bleak prospect: years of in-and-out shelter nipping.

23 August 1940

Last night there was a raid. WAAFs were woken by thuds of bombs and bursts of guns. One WAAF said, graphically, her whole house shook. Another saw shrapnel falling and the black swastikas of a German plane held in the searchlight's beam. Only I, of all the neighbours, went on sleeping, not a sound disturbed my admittedly agitated dreams of air raids, and not until, as is ever the case, half an hour after all the excitement was over and the sirens went off did I awake. Then, they were wailing in full horrid blast and Boompsie shouting, 'Joan, for God's sake wake up.' None of us could find our clothes; we rushed distractedly around, pulling on whatever we could find, quantities of strange and miscellaneous attire, and finally I followed my household to the shelter, wearing pyjamas, slacks, jumper, jacket, an old dirty but warm dressing gown, tennis shoes and carrying somehow two blankets, pillow, a gas mask, a tin hat and my anti-gas equipment. I secured a corner of the shelter, wrapped myself like a cocoon in the blankets and prepared for sleep when Boompsie unwisely said, 'We'd be caught like rats if we got a direct hit here' and that started me thinking about it. It isn't pleasant, even if the chances of that direct hit have been tactfully worked out by the daily press as several million to one.

We share a shelter with the airmen and their families from the married quarters. They have a lot of children. I saw a beloved baby in the arms of his mother, his sleepy lovely smiling face, vivid in the light of the hurricane lamp. He is such a beautiful baby, with large dark eyes and so many fair curls and his enchanting smile. It's so strange to think that we human beings are doing this to each other, which could include his wanton killing and has already included the killing of other people's babies. Fortunately what excitement there was, was over before we left our houses, the All Clear came and in some twenty minutes we were able to go back to bed. The morning showed us the bombs were dropped four or five miles away.

27 August 1940

The nights since I wrote this up last have been two or three times regularly broken with warnings. Nothing-fortunately-happening ones, but detrimental to our now much appreciated sleep, culminating in last night's utter limit of a warning, lasting six hours. I was over at the Goldies' as I had a day's leave and was thinking positive thoughts – such as the fact that I wouldn't have to spend a sleepless night in that bloody shelter. But the Goldies are nervous of raids and they refused to allow me to go to bed. At each distant bomb, at each overhead plane, we had to rush to their cupboard under the stairs – Mrs Goldie, Bunty, Bernie Brewer, I, three silly old ladies from the flat above with their corks and bits of cotton wool, Rex the dog and Tiny the kitten, which expressed what he thought of being cooped up in a cupboard by scratching Bernie sharply across the face and then escaping.

I was as angry as my need for sleep allowed me to be. I thought it so futile: we can't, I won't, spend years of my life clustered like bugs in some underground hideout. War it may be but I'm going to live my life still with some semblance of normality. When the bombs are on me then I'll go hide myself, but not just for all overcautious warnings like these last ones. So at twelve I said I just didn't care any more what happened to me, I had to go to sleep. Nothing in my life has ever been so exquisite as that moment of slipping in between the sheets. Out of the window I could see a vertical searchlight and overhead I could hear a plane which, by its engine's odd knocking, I surmised to be enemy. Utter weariness, however, I have discovered, is a perfect fear caster-outer. I turned over and went to sleep. The others huddled downstairs until the All Clear at four.

After a delightful day of shopping, spending all my

birthday money and buying a black costume and access- ories (clothes that aren't uniform are another thing I've learnt to appreciate), I am now here at Hendon early and about to sleep. I am officially on leave till twelve so if there's a warning before that I just won't go into the shelter. I'll dress, my furthermost concession to this war, and sleep in my clothes till bombs wake me. I washed clothes and mended clothes and boiled a sus- pender belt – all I know about boiling is that if you use Rinso you don't need to boil but I am experimenting. I am now going downstairs to eat what of my cake they left me after last night's 4 o'clock before going to bed guzzle. And then utter, utter joy, heavenly, rare, precious, appreciated bed.

2 September 1940

After a week of hell, at the end of which I sank so low as to sleep on the stony, unsympathetic, dusty floor of the shelter, the group captain, viewing his red-rimmed-eyed, exhausted officers, airmen and WAAFs, edicted that we no longer need take cover on red warnings but could wait till the Station broadcast called us privately to cover. So the sun is shining again and we sleep long uninterrupted nights and take absolutely no notice at all of the sirens, which continue to wail resentfully.

I cannot complain that life with my parents has been dull. I have never for more than a few years stayed in any one place. They are back in town, they have rented a house turned into service flatlets at the back of the

BBC, they live in a room at the top and a room in the basement. They have sold all their Claygate home and possessions with few exceptions, which include the oil painting of my mother which goes everywhere with us. Their tenants are BBC announcers and Polish refugees.

5 September 1940

On Tuesday I went for my Air Ministry Board with Priscilla Carpenter; I had the idea I didn't do so well. However, a fighter squadron has arrived at Hendon, making it operational and consequently more alive and exciting, and also many alluring Czechoslovakian pilots, so coupling these facts with home now being so near I shan't care too bitterly if I don't get it, provided I can successfully ward off the horror of being posted from here on a corporal's course.

Priscilla was in a very bad way. While at Hendon she fell in love with a flying officer, Bill, in Equipment section and he apparently fell in love with her. Matters were further complicated by the fact that she's already engaged to an Army officer of whom her family completely approve. Monday night's events were entangled further by Bill's being posted immediately to the Middle East. Priscilla wept all the night before her Board over him and later in her lonely bed, and all the next day, nearly over me. She says she can't live without him. I sympathised verbally all the time, but my brain was beastly, refusing to believe that this was really love and she couldn't have better controlled herself. My brain said dispassionately,

'She'll forget him when he's gone, she'll get over it.' Anyway, it's so silly making all this fuss. My brain is foul because I am fond of Priscilla; I have just become so cynical over love.

We ate the 1s 6d lunch in the Corner House Brasserie, Priscilla toying languidly with every course and I, not being in love, eating heartily my own lunch and most of hers. When we said goodbye she kissed me, nearly crying. I wanted to be sorry and give her all she wanted, but my brain thought, 'How silly we look, both in uniform, she a sergeant, kissing each other.'

Yesterday Joyce came over and we went out to have a meal at the Hendon Way. At the end of it a warning went and seeing flares being dropped in the aerodrome area I courageously said, 'It looks like Hendon's getting it, we'll stay here.' But whereas the first flare-dropping plane fulfilled its purpose, the following bombers were fortunately beaten back and for another night Hendon went untouched, no doubt the only aerodrome around this way to be so. During the meal Joyce said, 'Remember what we were talking about last time I was over?'

'You mean about sleeping with people and whether to or not?'

'Well, I have.'

She sat there, smiling and flourishingly attractive, and said it was marvellous and terrific fun. It's Johnny, the squadron leader she's been in love with since the beginning of the war. We were the two who said, 'How could people, we never would.' I envied her bitterly. I thought, 'She knows she's done it and nothing has altered about her at all.' I always did suspect a whole lot of hooey importance was placed on virginity.

7 September 1940

It is a war tonight. At five the first warning sounded. Pat Pell and I watched our Hurricane squadron taking off by hanging out of sickbay window which commands a view of a large piece of the drome. From where we hung we saw Hurricanes at every angle, taking off and landing, flying in formation, returning to refuel, dipping and twisting and rolling so near over our heads we felt that our upheld hands would scrape them. For variety there was the not so distant boom of guns and one very close burst of machine-gun fire.

When the All Clear went we waited and waited, but when we had counted in the last landing plane there were less than the twelve that went out. Later they told us two had not returned. This squadron has only just come, its pilots we don't know yet. When we do we'll wonder which of them hasn't come back when we count in their return. I am grateful I haven't a husband or a lover as a pilot, it must be apprehension all the time. I understand now why they are so hard and self-sufficient and untender; it's the only way they can endure living the way they have to live, each time going out with so little prospect of return.

At about eight the second warning went, in the London direction the sky was scarlet, the police on the gate told us that the London docks were burning. Then the guns sounded and searchlights went up, silver strips across the glow in the sky, weird and beautiful; the night is beginning now, it's clear and starry and raids will go on till dawn.

15 September 1940

Summary of so many days – days with so much in them happening I had no time to describe them. Here and now that they have passed, I have space only for snatches.

The first night of the London barrage of guns booming and roaring with the whole earth shaking, and shrapnel falling and I alone in this mad wild world.

Sitting seeing *Irene* with Boompsie and Molly and sighing for past gentler days and hating the present crudity of life, war having ripped away its covering frills; weeping at the screen desolation of London.

Last night, Molly and I had been taken to the pictures by a corporal of her section whose wife is ill in hospital and who wanted cheering up. After, he had to go on duty, so we got him to drop us at the Hendon Way[34] as Molly had had no tea. We had eaten a decorous sandwich at the snack bar and we were on our way out when some officers of 24 Squadron, there with their wives and girlfriends, asked us to have a drink with them before we went.

Then in came three of our new fighter boys, enor-

[34] The Hendon Way was a popular rendezvous, a restaurant and bar, packed at this time with servicemen and women. It still exists today.

mously tall, incredibly handsome and by themselves. There was a dance on upstairs and the officers giving us drinks made these three come and join our party and we all went up to the dance.

I did have such fun. I danced mostly with a tall, thin, ugly-attractive one called Norman Hunt.[35] It got hot and we went and stood on the balcony to watch the moon. He played gently with my hair and it was peaceful and pleasant and I amused, contented and unaroused. After a while I said, 'Let's go back to the dance' and we did. He dances well, not as sublimely as Sam did, but I enjoyed it. Then we went back to drink, Molly and I surrounded by the three of them, Michael and John and Norman, all so colossally tall.

At twelve the dance ended and Norman brought me home. At my gate I made him go early. He lifted me up in his arms and held me so that I could not escape him. 'No, let me go, it's late, there's plenty more time for us to be together.'

'Not so nice as this time, meeting you for the first time,' so we made a date for Monday night.

16 September 1940

It's Monday evening now, with me sitting half dressed in preparedness for going out.

Already one of them is dead: John[36], who was large

---

[35] Norman Hunt was killed in the Battle of Britain, 1940.
[36] John Gurteen.

and tall and young and so very attractive. John who called me 'pie face' and when I protested went down on his knees and called me his 'darling love'; who flicked my nose and said I should not have such an absurd one. Oh, the wicked, pointless destroying of life.

17 September 1940

I met Norman at the station last night, in the inevitable barrage of guns, and we went on to the Hendon Way. Four of his officers were there and we joined them. They talked to me and bought me drinks and gave me cigarettes. I thought they were somewhat apathetic about my presence.

Then about seven sergeant pilots from the same squadron swelled our ring. I went down with them far more successfully beginning to enjoy the evening, as most women would, the only girl with so many men. At 10.30 the bar closed so we went back into the other room where we could drink till 11.30 if we all ate sandwiches.

While the sergeant played the piano others stood round him singing. They tried to persuade me to give up the squadron's officers in their favour and go with them to the Sergeants Dance but at 11.30 Norman and I left them.

At the roundabout he said, 'Where to now? Town?' Some sense in me still declined so he said, 'As we're in no hurry we'll walk home.' It was a clear and lovely night and the guns then were spasmodic. We walked along the empty streets, the only people in the world. He left me at my gate at half past two and we made a date for Wednesday.

19 September 1940

The guns were going again when I met Norman at the station last night. It had been a horrible day, hearing the adjutant arrange the collection of John's body; hearing from girls back from town about the gutting of Oxford Street stores; wondering during each of the eight warnings whether this time Norman, like John, would die.

Again, we went to the Hendon Way and again most of 504 Squadron were there. The officers I already knew welcomed me with a friendly warmth and straight away I knew the evening was going to be fun. After a while we went again into the other room where again one of the sergeants played for us and the others sat round drinking and laughing and asking Norman in turn whether they could dance with me. Then for the last half-hour, again sleepy and content, I sat with Norman and Mickey and laughed with them. Mickey is enormous and mad, always in a muddle, laughing at himself with much too much charm.

At quarter to twelve Norman and I went home and held close to each other under an arch in the darkness, I thinking unhappily how wonderful this moment would be if he had a future like normal men, not going so many times each day to a death which today or tomorrow will claim him.

I never can enjoy just the moment nor ever forget the

ruthless rush of time. At my billet he kissed me and said, 'I'll see you tomorrow at the dance.' That is the Sergeants Dance tomorrow evening, all his squadron are going and so will be all the WAAFs.

24 September 1940

Molly came along to my office and said, 'One of the men in Signals says he'll take us to see the bomb damage in Hendon, he's got a car,' and as I had nothing else to do I went.

There wasn't much to see at Hendon, so he said, 'I'll take you to Kilburn, you'll really see something then.'

BB Evans, where I used to buy my school hats, hadn't a window in the place. Opposite, what had been a row of shops was a pile of rubble. In the next street stood empty houses, their windows broken, their curtains blown in half, their doors down and their porches battered.

We went into a Lyons opposite and had tea, according to the waitress we hadn't seen anything. We should go to Kensal Rise, where a landmine had come down, where three hundred people had been killed, where streets of houses had vanished from existence.

We went to see what we could but the area was pretty effectively roped off. Up one street we could see a row of houses looking as broken and bedraggled as if some giant had shaken them.

So Molly and I, all the way back in the car, back to where our driver had got us to a cinema, said we'd never

never grumble any more about being fed up, life being dull at Hendon. We're alive, the visit did us good.

When we came out we were cold and hungry and all the shops were shut in Golders Green, so we decided to go to Henri's in Hendon, racing quickly to the station, looking occasionally at a searchlight-laden sky in apprehension that perhaps a landmine on a beastly green parachute[37] might be descending on our tin hats.

At the station we passed an RAF officer paying for a ticket he hadn't taken. He took each of us by an arm and said, 'Hello, girls, fancy seeing you here.' It was Mac, he was young and fair and trying to grow a moustache. He was going to the Hendon Way to meet another officer, newly posted to the squadron, and said, 'Come along with me.' Red was the new officer, he was small and stocky with auburn hair and when we arrived he was pretty drunk. He was nineteen last month, he'd been all through France and has eight Germans to his credit. It's so pathetic all the experience and emotion being thrust on children in a year so that they know at nineteen what they should have taken till twenty-one to learn gently.

I was cold and rude and uninterested and made him mad. We came home together, Mac and Molly walking contentedly some yards in front of us. Neither his anger nor his endearments could move me. He was a ridiculous years-older-than-I-am child.

We sat on the doorstep smoking and listening to the

[37] The Germans used landmines attached to parachutes before V2s.

guns and because I never will learn not to tell the truth, I told him about Norman. He said, 'You're sure to come up against it sooner or later, some fighter pilot after your body.' He laughed and smiled. 'Joan, I don't want your body, if I did I'd tell you straight away.' He shivered. 'Sorry it's a bad habit of mine, shivering: nerves I guess.'

He said I had to get over Norman and get over him quickly because he wanted to be the next to take his place.

He persuaded me to meet him at nine o'clock tonight and go with him to the Hendon Way.

26 September 1940

I didn't go after all, that evening, I mean. I was very tired and when it got to nine, the guns were going louder and nearer and more steadily than usual. Then at 9.05, with my mind still undecided, a fanfare blew because incendiary bombs had dropped on the embankment at the other end of the aerodrome. And when I came out of the shelter at 9.45 I went unguiltily and gratefully to bed.

The next morning I phoned to apologise and explain, learning that he had waited half an hour, and we made another date for that night. Now I have to write down about that night and the hours after it – a mad, fantastic and impossible period that I know just couldn't have been real.

Molly and I met Mac and Red at Hendon at nine and went as ever to the Hendon Way. I'd got the miseries so

Red gave me Pimm's to drink and as that made me worse, some unknown drink guaranteed by him to cheer up even me: it certainly wuzzed my head up. We danced a little, we sat around talking and laughing and at the end of the evening clustered round Scruffy at the piano while he played and we sang sentimental songs. Occasionally a bomb fell so near the walls and windows of the Winter Garden rattled furiously. When you're pretty drunk you just don't care.

At 11.30 Red said, 'I'm suddenly very old and tired, let's go home,' and home we started for, Molly and I wearing their flying jackets and they carrying our gas masks and gas equipment for us.

At the station we were told we could get neither Tube, bus nor taxi and Colindale they told us was flattened out. At the time it didn't really register and we started to walk back up the hill.

Mac and Red had to be on duty at dawn. A few yards up a bomb fell nastily near. Red pushed me to the ground and crouched beside me. It sobered me up quite a lot, but drink certainly is quite a wonderful fear deadener.

Then the shrapnel started to fall and from the top of the hill we could see the aerodrome burning abandonedly. Red said, 'I think we ought to get to a shelter,' so the four of us walked over a field to a shelter, and, when we entered it the startled inhabitants sat and regarded Molly and my leather-jacketed, tin-hatted strangeness and said, 'Are you Germans?'

When we explained they let us stay there, giving us one inadequate blanket which supplemented the jackets we prepared to sleep on. Red behaved beautifully, only once he kissed my unresponsive lips, and then said, 'Sorry, I forgot you didn't want it.' I didn't either, although I liked him a lot, he was fun, he had personality, he was alive. Mostly we lay and giggled and fought Molly and Mac for a share of the blanket and tried, without much success, to sleep. I guess we were pretty pesky to the rest of the inhabitants.

At 4.30 Mac said we had to go so we climbed out of the skylight to save waking the rest of the shelter by scrabbling across them. The fire on the drome had vanished and we started our walk back.

Walking down Aerodrome Road, we saw them extinguishing part of the fire and we all four of us walked into the hoses. Wet and cold and tousled, we parted at the aerodrome gate with the warden on duty telling us of a landmine which had wiped out Colindale Station and caused numerous deaths.

The morning was even more fantastic. There was a scar at the airmen's entrance of Station Headquarters where an incendiary bomb had fallen. There were the Orderly Room boys with their horrible tales of helping sort out the broken-up bodies, buried under the wrecked Tube station. And then Molly came in and said, 'They're going, they've been posted at an hour's notice, 504 Squadron, Joan.'

A few minutes later we saw all sixteen Hurricanes flying in formation across the aerodrome and out of our lives. Molly was nearly crying. Mac was very sweet. I wouldn't ever love Red but he stood for some little security and now he too is gone. If only life would stop this dreadful rushing and move just a little more slowly. My emotions just won't react any more to all that is happening to me.

28 September 1940

Yesterday, directly work had ended, Molly and I went to Brent to the pictures. Colindale Station is working again and we saw it for the first time. It made my stomach sick. Its booking offices and shops and telephone booths and massive concrete roof and pillars just weren't there any more.

Between the battered bank and window-shattered houses was a horrible pile of brick and rubble with underneath it still, they told us, people buried.

Over at Brent where we went to the cinema was the same sight: blocks of flats piled up in rubble, glassless windows, battered roofs. The cinema was nearly empty and the programme ended at just after eight. When we came out the guns were going and the sudden shrill wail of the sirens started, making us duck groundward, holding each other's hand saying, 'A bomb.' That other awful night had tested our nerves. 'It isn't any good,' I said to Molly, 'I'll walk five miles but I won't go back to that station.' It wasn't the thought that they'd hit it again, it was the horrible nightmarish thought of the sight of it. So we stopped a passing van, which kindly gave us a lift back to the aerodrome.

30 September 1940

I write this in bed by candlelight, outside the inevitable crump of the guns. This has been a day. It began at breakfast by Miss Clough (admin officer) saying no clean sheets because we might have to leave our billets to make room for incoming airmen.

All the morning we passed to each other the wildest of wild rumours: we were going to be moved out that night, we were going to be billeted in council houses among slum clearance people and bugs. They would march us early in the morning from billets to Mess.

At lunchtime Miss Clough told us we would have to be in new billets by the following evening and that she was spending the afternoon with a policeman finding them for us.

3 October 1940

Oh, the unmitigated hell of the last three days! It's been raining nearly all the time and very cold, enough anyway to make us remember the horror of last winter, which the sun in the summer helped us forget. And though I ask for them in every letter, Mother still hasn't sent my vests and I've lost both my pairs of woollen gloves.

They still won't tell us whether or not we're to be billeted out. Fighter Command and our squadron admin are fighting bitterly about it and until someone decides something, all of us live in nasty, dingy, empty rooms, furnished only by suitcases and kitbags because we've got to be ready to leave at a minute's notice, and at nights we sleep and itch on sheetless beds. This war is beastly enough as it is, without additional inconveniences being put upon us.

I think of all of it what I hate most of all is the blackout. From 7.30 onwards now you stumble around in total darkness. If you do go out there's nothing to do except go to the pictures with another WAAF and walk home in blackness with an air raid on and guns going. It didn't matter when 504 were here because of course we had them to come home with. And with them and drinks inside us we weren't afraid. Now they've gone and there's no new squadron and it's too dangerous to go up to town at nights. And all we get is work in the day and being cold and guns and bombs and blackout at nights. With all my friends never seen any more and my parents evacuated, it's a lousy war and to emphasise its lousiness, one of the corporals who was in the WACs[38] in the last war, told us tales this afternoon of life with that in France. Apparently it was one long round of fun, with interesting work and hundreds of fascinating officers to take you out and shower you with presents.

However, I think I've passed my peak of misery. Joyce came over at lunchtime today and seeing her cheered me a little. We sat in her car and ate chocolate caramels, which I adore, and talked about her Johnny. After tea there was a letter from Eric and tonight he phoned.

[38] Women's Army Corps.

I told him just how miserable I was and wallowed in his sympathy. It's comforting to know someone does sincerely mind what happens to you, after all these dashing-and-don't-care-a-damn-for-you-except-for-your-body, for-the-moment, pilots.

6 October 1940

Molly and I took a day's leave together yesterday. We took a bus to Selfridges, hanging from the window in horror at the desolation of Oxford Street. It was dreadful to see the ruins of John Lewis and to think of the money lost to its and other big store owners. They were such large, rich, beautiful, solid stores. It's getting a familiar if still horrible sight these days. A road as normal as sanity and then suddenly, dreadfully, as a dream, a smashed and broken building.

Afterwards we went to the pictures, coming out to go and have a drink at the American Bar at the Regent Palace and to wish we could think of someone to take us out that evening so that we hadn't to go back to our stripped, comfortless billet. Just as we rose reluctantly, to be back at Hendon before dark and air raids, the major in a party of officers to our right said to us, 'Please don't walk out on us like that, have a drink with us before you go.' So we had a drink. Next we had another drink. Then the major said to two young lieutenants, 'We have to go now, we'll leave you to look after these two WAAFs,' and shaking us warmly by the hand, left us. The two remaining lieutenants were brothers called Tony and Noel, and while they went to buy our third drink we said, 'I wonder what now?' 'Let's stay a while and see,' said Molly and, thinking distastefully of the foul return journey, I agreed.

They were nice unwarlike-looking boys just out of the hospital with BEF[39] evacuation wounds. We went to the Queens to eat, drinking vin rouge, leaning smilingly against the restaurant's padded walls and listening to the band's gentle, sentimental music. The Queens bar is a friendly place with all its customers in uniform. A party of RAF and naval officers urged us to join them in their quest for further fun, and sitting up at the bar, Paul Dickson and Maclead, two Hendon officers and very drunk, tried to persuade us to go with them to the Coconut Club. We rejected both offers and took a taxi to No. 8 Hallam Street,[40] for Molly and me to spend the night there. By that time it was past twelve and the guns and bombs were going in persistent unison. Hallam Street is empty now, except for Mitchell, the caretaker in the basement, so we offered the boys beds there for the night.

In our bedroom, Molly and I pooled our beauty resources for the morning – I had hairpins and she lent me her net. We had powder and lipstick and rouge but no mascara, so I could only wash up to my eyes so as still to have black eyebrows in the morning. After a bath they got pretty pale but I restored them with a brainwave and lead pencil.

Now it's the next evening and we're sitting tired in our

[39] British Expeditionary Force.
[40] My parents' house near the BBC.

billets, with Mrs Wright (WAAF CO), being told we missed church parade and will more than likely be put on charge. Oh, well, let them, yesterday would be worth it.

7 October 1940

Last night I was on guardroom duty, a boring two hours which I passed knitting a glove, drinking soup and grapefruit squash and watching other WAAFs play very good table tennis. An hour before I had been playing hockey for the second time in my life and WAAF career and basking in the satisfaction of having scored three goals. We are so used now to guns and bombs that nothing louder or nearer than usual registers on our overworked ears, and going back to my billet in a momentary lull, I thought, 'Hurrah, a quieter night,' and went to investigate my bath prospects. Consequently I was annoyed to hear the fanfare and surprised to see enormous flames leaping very near. They told us 234 Squadron had been hit. If a year ago any part of the aerodrome had been hit we would have gone mad with panic. Now only the bombs actually on us ring any excitement from our exhausted emotions.

We were in the shelter for three hours, I dozing in that now perpetual state of mind that can see no further than the actual moment and has lost all its capabilities for exhaustion and imagination. In the morning we learnt that about twelve training planes, quantities of documents and several hangars had been gutted. We learnt also that German and Italian troops were in Romania.

9 October 1940

I think the last twenty-three hours have been the most horrible of my life. They bombed us again last night. I was warm in bed with a book and a bottle, some chocolates and a fire, when the first bomb fell. I think it hit the other side of our road. By the time I had leapt from bed to my pile of shelter clothing, two more had fallen further up Booth Road. Then there was a lull and no fanfare sounded, the excitement, I supposed, was over and because I hate the shelter and my bed was warm I went back into it.

Suddenly the two bombs fell. The noise was louder than anything I had ever heard, I thought it had broken my ears. For an endless time I heard their awful whistle and rush as they descended. I was too dazed and bewildered to think or act coherently. I put my face in the pillow, pulled the blankets over my head and waited, whimpering, for the crash. On the second bomb, the lights too went out. I leapt from bed to the accompanying sound of falling plaster and breaking glass and looked out of the window. The bomb had fallen directly in line with my house, not fifty yards the other side of the fence, hitting the electric generator of the camp, which was lighting the drome with blue and orange flames. I waited no longer but snatched some clothes, my tin hat and my diaries and fled to the shelter, arriving there as the fanfare sounded. In the shelter Molly was pouring salva latterly[41]

---

[41] Sal Volatile. The name of a syrup that soothed the nerves.

down the protesting throat of a hysterical WAAF. Then another WAAF, much shaken, stumbled in. She'd just missed the bomb down the road and her tin hat had stood between her head and several bricks.

The fanfare period was over by half past nine and most of us went back to bed, our sleep shattered by guns and luckily a little more distant bombs. It happened so suddenly and was over so swiftly it's difficult to realise now that it happened, except that my nerves tonight are lousy.

After a miserable day with an aching head, Molly said to me, 'Joan, isn't it dreadful, one of the men in Accounts told me today that seven of 504's officers have been killed since they left here.' Seven of them: that's nearly all of the officers. It made me sick with shock.

I went to play hockey after but I could only look up at the red beauty of the sky and remember the fortnight they were here. It's the wicked, pointless dreadfulness of their deaths; they haven't had any life at all. Old people dying isn't so dreadful, but they had a right to years of living, to homes and wives and families and peaceful, lasting, solid days. How can any of them be blamed for their ruthless living, their desperate cramming of every sensation into hours when, instead of the gentle years, they have only the rushing days?

13 October 1940

We have a new group captain here and the first day he came to power he put all the local haunts out of bounds to WAAFs with officers. At the moment I don't care; we haven't any decent squadrons here anyway but if the future brings them it's going to possibly cramp our style. In all other respects he looks a very decent sort of person so I can't hate him with the wholeheartedness I'd like to.

Molly and I, if it pans out the way I want it, are going up to Cheltenham on a week's leave on Monday so that we can have a last desperate fling before we have to behave ourselves as prospective admin corporals.

18 October 1940

The colour of my days! Joyce is back at Hendon in what I trust will only be a temporary disgrace. While out on a run, she forgot to take a spare wheel, got a puncture and she and her passenger were obliged to return in a milk van. Unfortunately her passenger was an air vice marshal.

Part of a letter from Mother describing her new job:

Some of the dear old Cheltenham dames who chat
to me about the terrible refugees from London,
little think I am one of them. Last week I had a
dame who must have been about seventy, trying on
a smart young silk frock. She had gaiters almost up
to her knees and thin long flannel bloomers which
almost met the top of the gaiters when she took off
her frock and all the time she was trying on frocks
she was worried about her wretched hair net which

all the time got tangled up in a zip fastener. After getting her unravelled I had to leave the fitting room to get my face straight.

I am proud of my mother, she's got guts.

22 October 1940

On Monday night our leave began. Molly and I struggled with our cases and our coats and our gas masks up to town to Joyce's flat where we were spending the night. The flat, shared by Joyce and another WAAF, had no water, a musty smell and a lot of dirty washing up. So we dropped our luggage and went round to the nearest pub. After a scratchy but good supper of soup and bread and marmalade and beer, all three of us slept in her large double bed, not much disturbed by falling bombs.

23 October 1940

Now we come to our Cheltenham adventure.

We caught the train at two o'clock from Paddington, departing in an air raid and arriving here, after one hell of a journey, at twenty minutes to eight. Mother was nobly waiting to meet us and thrust us onto our bus with airy talk of the warmth and comfort and joy that awaited us in a delightful hostel full of Cambridge students, so our hearts rose, only to fall on entering a large lino-covered wooden hall: the living room of our hostel.

A too bright little woman led us to our beds, she opened

the door of a dingy dormitory and led us to two bunks, built on the principle of the air raid shelter bunk bed, handed us a pile of blankets and a beastly sleeping bag sheet affair, waved a hand towards a row of tin basins and cold water and left us to make our own beds.

We looked at the room and the lino and the drabness and the hooks on the walls for our clothes and remembering our journey – visions of cosy little rooms, water-bottle-lined beds, breakfast brought to us, warm large fires – laughed so hysterically that I thought we should never stop. Supper was served sitting on a wooden bench before a wooden table, with what fire there was hidden by many layers of evacuees and in the company of several earnest cyclists, healthily packed into awful shorts and obviously registering us as hopeless sissies. In bed we couldn't even say what we thought about it all as the dormitory was shared by a particularly hearty and revolting female cyclist. Breakfast conversation consisted of social welfare in the slums and after breakfast tasks were allotted to us and sullenly, bitterly and this was our seven days' leave thoughts, Molly and I washed up. Our thoughts were united: get out of this!

24 October 1940

Cheltenham adventures – second instalment.

After the washing up we hitch-hiked to the town, our faces shining with purpose, to find a fresh billet. We tried the YWCA, which appeared to consist of an unhelpful and superior band of women (Cheltenham is full of them, well-bred, haughty, bound in by the complicated code of their caste).

Next we went to the WVS,[42] there they were considerably more helpful, giving us the address of a village in Gotheringham where there might be a room and there immediately we hitch-hiked.

The owner of Pear Tree Cottage is a funny, talkative, tiny, kind little woman whose husband died last August. For five shillings a week we sleep in her warm double feather bed, cook our own food over her fire and gather in the evenings before its warmth. There is neither gas nor electric light nor bath nor lavatory and the floors downstairs are stone flagged. Still, she gives us hot-water bottles and an endless chain of cups of tea, and from our window we can see the Cotswold Hills.

After the last entry there is a gap of four months. During that time I travelled to Exeter, met Red again, fell in love and had a brief affair, which was soon ended by him. Much later on I tore out and destroyed the relevant pages.

[42] Women's Voluntary Service.

Events of 1940

1 January Two million British men were called up to fight.

8 January Butter, bacon and sugar became the first products to be rationed in Britain.

9 April Germany invaded Norway and Denmark, bringing 'The Phoney War' to an end.

30 April A German bomber crashed into housing, causing the first deaths on the British mainland.

10 May Winston Churchill became Prime Minister; German troops invaded Holland, Belgium and France.

14 May 250,000 men signed up to join the Home Guard.

26 May The evacuation of Dunkirk began. Over eight days 300,000 defeated British and French troops were removed from French beaches.

30 May The British government ordered the removal of all signposts and street names as a precaution against invasion.

10 June Italy declared war on Britain and France.

22 June After the fall of Paris, France surrendered to Germany.

30 June Germany occupied the Channel Islands, reaching the very doorstep of the British mainland.

3 July The British Navy sunk the French fleet at port in Algeria, drowning 1300 French sailors.

10 July The Battle of Britain began.

1 August Hitler announced plans for the invasion of Britain.

7 September The Blitz began with a daylight raid on the East End.

14 November Coventry was flattened in a 13-hour raid.

29 December German bombers started 'The Second Great Fire of London', blowing out the central water mains when the Thames was at its lowest.

1941

2 February 1941

Dancing with Eric at the Hendon Way, my face aching with its effort at gaiety because he must never suspect about Red. And hearing him say, 'It was your looks which first attracted me to you' and feeling gratitude and then pity after I had asked him why he wanted to transfer from Army to Air Force: 'It's all I want to do now, anyway, live for the day.' I think of how it was all such a stupid waste of love: Eric loving me and me loving Red and Red loving only Red.

Leaning my head against the wall of the cloakroom while Molly powdered her beautiful and uneeding it face, torn with pain because I couldn't push away the strangers outside nor push back the days until it was September again, with Red and Mac and the rest of them outside, Red holding my hand as we sat by the piano. Red screwing up his eyes when he smiled, Red everywhere. 'Yes I know you don't like public demonstrations of affection.' And when we asked the pianist to play ''Fools Rush in'', she said it was getting out of date. Seeing Eric to the station, smiling, self-assured and poised, walking home with

Molly and suddenly beginning to weep so that I couldn't stop until we were almost home. Going out with Molly, Peter and Alex, who used to be in Shell, sitting with them in the cinema and regretting the normalness of days, the absence of that heady illusion of glamour Red gave to living, eating chicken sandwiches and drinking whisky and ginger wine in pubs with them and wondering why there was no excitement left at all.

9 February 1941

I went home this weekend to my parents in Cheltenham. It began badly by seeing, as I walked across Paddington Station to the Cheltenham train, the Exeter train and having to watch it go out. There was nothing to stop me from getting on it, phoning when I got there and saying, 'Red, I'm here,' except the actual physical restraint. I got onto my own train and read myself into a headache.

My parents gave me a wonderful day. We had coffee in a Cheltenham café, we had drinks in the Royal Bar and lunch with wine at the Royal Hotel, only on the way there we passed the Plough and the Plough is another memory of Red, and an RAF officer in the bar had hair like Red's and the same sort of face.

In the afternoon we saw Tom Walls in *Canaries Sometimes Sing* at the Opera House and in the evening after a meal we sat by the fire, listening to the life of Marie Lloyd.

I hope they enjoyed their day; I am wishing now that

I could have been gayer. And back in my room at night, I saw him sleeping in our Exeter bed with his bony nose and his wide mouth and his sleepy scowl, so pathetically touching and young. I remembered his two dreadful sentences which I never will forget: 'Don't fall for me, Joan, I'm a bad type, don't get too much of a crush on me, will you, darling.'

All the way back in the train I thought – I love him. Even knowing all his faults and realising that he has ditched me, I still cannot stop my love.

12 February 1941

Back at Hendon. The Lockharts[43] are organising concerts and drama leagues and variety acts and even producing someone to teach ballroom dancing. Already such stars as Edith Evans and Dorothy Dickson have been because of them to Hendon. They must be a more than welcome pair to the people who come into the Air Force from being actors and producers and playwrights and press agents.

Molly and I, more or less by accident, got in with the drama league and stayed in it at first because Molly thought doing as many things as we could would be quite an idea for both of us and later because we liked it. Its principal pillars besides Mrs Bruce Lockhart are two members of the Hendon Ground Defence, Howard

---

[43] Bruce Lockhart ran the YMCA in Hendon; his wife was an actress before the war.

Marion Crawford and Ashley Bartlett, the first an ex-actor, broadcaster, the second an ex-journalist.

Marion Crawford is large and fair and very very funny. He made me laugh till I cried, I am deeply grateful to him for that. I haven't laughed so much for such ages and I felt so very much better after it. It's impossible now to go on seeing myself as a tragedy queen; it's put a lot of things into their proper perspective. It's made me see what a rich long length of life I have and the proportion of certain incidents in that stretch. He made us laugh about so many things, he can't be described as a completely successful airman; he doesn't take the Air Force with any seriousness.

27 February 1941

This afternoon was fun. We got off from work at three o'clock to go to the YMCA to rehearse for Tuesday. For the first hour I sat watching singers, dancers and comedians with Mrs Lockhart and Marion Crawford prompting and producing, and Ashley Bartlett with a watch on the table timing the turns. The war was a million miles away.

Then everyone else went home and we went into the quiet room to rehearse our sketch. Afterwards we came out and sat round a table laughing a lot and drinking countless cups of very dark tea: it was such fun and I hope so much that the show is a success.

Now I'm in my billet, toying with a few of the many pressing household tasks and the idea of whether or not to go later to a dance at Hendon Hall.

1 March 1941

We've been rehearsing all this week: last night from seven until after ten, Marion Crawford producing and flogging our emotions with such a ruthlessness that we came back to bed exhausted. As a producer he's a fiend, as a man he's an angel. I don't think anyone could help but adore him, I haven't met anyone like him before in my life and I'll never, never cease to be grateful to him for that evening when I thought I should die of misery and he made me laugh.

Tonight we rehearsed the Collar sketch, which was Bartlett and Biddy and I, and Marion Crawford producing.

6 March 1941

Tuesday was one of those days with a lot of things happening in them. I had an Air Ministry Board in the morning at eleven so didn't get up at the usual dawn-beastliness and instead of working went up to town. The Board went very well and I think I passed it, except that they want me to have a photographic interpretation commission, instead of the code and cipher one I was trying for. Photographic interpretation is far more interesting work but a hellishly stiff test has to be passed before it's given you, and that's where I may well come undone. If I do get through though, life should be very good: I'll have interesting and worthwhile work at last.

At Adastral House I met another WAAF corporal who

was up with me at our mutual Boards six months ago, so we went out to lunch together, taking ourselves to Hatchetts and spending £1 between us on a beautiful, heavenly pre-war-sort-of-food lunch.

Then at 2.30 p.m. we reluctantly left and parted at the Empire, she to see *Philadelphia Story* and I to go back to Hendon (not to work: I hadn't any intention of doing that).

31 March 1941

The gap in this was caused as last year by the measles, only this time it was the English and not the German variety, and have they been hell!

I spent the first three days of them in the WAAFs sickbay, labelled with influenza, with a temperature beginning at 101 and rising to a horrid climax of 104 in the company of Ozzie, a WAAF officer who makes toy animals and is kind and fun and is suffering from shock as a result of being in the Café de Paris bombing.

Then the rash began to come and, feeling too awful to describe, I have been sent to Colindale Hospital, where at intervals during the night doctors scratched and prodded my weary reflexes to see whether I had got CSM.[44]

The next morning saw my rash in full unbelievable song, so another nurse appeared and another ambulance, and I was taken, feeling even iller, to the Hampstead Fever Hospital.

[44] Cerebrospinal meningitis.

There I languished for a long weary week, firstly in a ward with thirty bawling brats – an experience which has soured me as a confirmed child hater. For a whole day and an even longer night these unmentionable howlers kept me awake. Oh, the monotony of the nerve-rawing repetition of a crying child!

I thought of wild desperate plans to escape, only I hadn't any clothes and was much too ill to move. I was trapped and helpless and desperate and despairing.

And then fortunately they moved me into a side ward with only one other silent little boy. I began to feel better and excruciatingly bored. I couldn't have visitors, I read so quickly I exhausted their meagre supplies and their food was foul. So I raised such hell to get out that they liberated me, still infectious according to the horror-stricken medical officer at Hendon on my return, several days earlier than they had intended. In return for which I unwisely parted with a pint of blood to be inoculated with children suspected of measles, to help them have it less severely.

After all this I really wasn't feeling so good and had to see Molly go without me to a party, with Bones[45] and his wife, and turn down a date with Eric and a date with John Carr, an officer I met at a Hendon dance on the Friday before the measles blow, to go miserably to bed at eight o'clock.

The next day I limped up here to Liverpool to spend my two weeks' sick leave with my relations.

[45] Marion Crawford was nicknamed Bones because of his big build.

After a week of sleeping for hours and having breakfast in bed, I feel all I was before again and my restlessness is back. I've got my commission, at least I've passed my Board and will get it as soon as my training's done. And when I go back of course I really will be leaving Hendon and I don't know at all where my new life will take me. I'll be sorry to go but it's best to leave on a peak, not linger past the prime so that in the staleness you forget the happy parts. The eighteen months at Hendon will be, I think, among the most vital in my life, they've changed me more fully than I could ever have believed possible.

17 April 1941

There was one hell of a raid on London last night. The warning went at 8.30 p.m. and from then until ten o'clock wave after wave of planes passed over us. The next morning, the rest of the WAAFs were full of the awful night it had been, with colossal gunfire and nearby bombs and weird flashes and falling shrapnel and flares, and all the accompaniments to a really top form air raid, so it was like it was last September, even complete with a fire. Personally, I don't know anything about it because I was asleep. This wasn't bravery only tiredness, and one of my accomplishments won after these months of blitzes is an ability to go on sleeping no matter how loud the noise. Besides, if a bomb does hit the house, if I'm in bed or cowering awake afraid under the stairs, I'll still be killed, and if I've got to be one of them, I'd rather be asleep at the time.

In the morning there weren't any papers. I had heard the seven o'clock news in that dulled, unlistening state of not being really awake and having to compress, as I do every morning, some forty minutes of washing, dressing and room tidying into twenty. Later, we heard all sorts of startling rumours and even later, the most startling news was confirmed about the West End damage – in places we know very well like the Queens Restaurant and the Empire Cinema. It's not only a building that's destroyed but all the things you did in them and all those hours spent there gone too.

30 April 1941

I spent twenty-four hours' leave yesterday with Joyce and it wasn't any fun at all. She took me with some other of her friends to a party at the Mayfair. We drank and we ate and we danced. One was a WAAF from Air Ministry Transport like Joyce. She was twenty-two, had married at eighteen and divorced at twenty. She was about as sophisticated as they come. Another was a large, too rich, conceited civilian whom I hated so violently I had to keep on thinking 'this is Joyce's friend and I am her guest' not to be rude to him. Another was a group captain – who reminded me why we're on the way to losing the war: he was characterless, negative, unintelligent and dim. None of them had anything to talk about. I didn't belong; I didn't want to belong; I didn't try to belong (which I was pleased about). I sat there and watched them drinking too much whisky and wished it was time to go home.

At three we left and went to the Piccadilly Lyons Corner House, eating Welsh rarebit and waffles and drinking coffee. The people there were more interesting to look at and listen to than the Mayfair bunch: chorus girls with inky black hair, phoney eyelashes, phoney glamour and looking like they needed a wash, with much-smaller-than-themselves boyfriends with bright suits and an equal absence of cleanliness.

It was four before we got back to Joyce's flat and the dawn was already a bar of light across the night-covered-up sky.

We slept till eleven, which made us too late to order breakfast, so I sat up in bed and read the *Daily Express*, which I had bought hours earlier in the Corner House. That was the first time in my life I had bought a morning paper before going to bed.

Then that drippy group captain phoned us up. He had left some pilot officer in charge of his department where I can't imagine he's ever needed. He proposed to waste the country's money some more by taking us out for the day, so we had lunch with him and sat in the Stalls of some dreary musical show with him and drank Pimm's at the RAF Club and ate supper at Kensington Close with him and then I left Joyce and came back here, grateful for the sight of Molly and Boomps.

11 May 1941

In this utterly satisfactory moment I am lying in slacks and open shirt on an eiderdown in the garden,

Boompsie's wireless by my head and my bare feet in the grass. I have a lot of work to do: I should be learning how to identify German and Italian aircraft. You see, at last my course has come through. I go to Marlow for a fortnight on Monday, on a photographic interpretation course. It should be interesting, if difficult, and it's the beginning of my escape from Hendon.

PART II

Medmenham

1941

12 May 1941

So here I am at Medmenham. Molly came to the station to see me off. Beyond feeling slightly sickish after breakfast I have no other feeling about leaving.

When I got out of the train at Marlow the oddness of it began. I asked the stationmaster how I got to Medmenham. He said everyone phoned for transport which I took a very good view of. I waited about ten minutes for my prospective transport and then instead of a car or even a lorry came a dashing young sergeant on a motorbike and sidecar – into the latter of which he fitted me, my suitcase, my respirator and tin hat. Then we bowled at a delightful speed along country lanes to Danesfield: an enormous building along the abbey/castle lines which the RAF have recently commandeered.

The sergeant took me to the Orderly Room where I gave out copious particulars. A lance-corporal took me to Accounts and I gave out some more. A WAAF officer took me to our room, which is bleak, pretty dirty and generally comfortless and got to by climbing up a lighthouse-like staircase. It has a bathroom attached, which would be a better idea if the water were any more than merely tepid.

There I met one of my co-course mates, Helga, an earnest female and one of the industrious and utterly uninspiring types. She says prayers at night; still I admire her moral courage in doing that.

Then we went to tea. We feed in an ante-room of the airmen's cookhouse, sharing it with the sergeants whose Mess isn't yet ready. Apparently the idea is to stagger us but we don't acknowledge RAF procedures with such familiarity. We were told at first that we had breakfast before the sergeants, before 7.30 a.m.; we said we'd rather not and fixed it for 8.30 a.m., a great improvement on Hendon.

After tea we went to see the flight sergeant disciplinary, to learn the 'whys' and 'whats' of the rules. There appear to be very few; we shall do what we like anyway, we're the only three WAAF cadets here, all the others are officers and the late passes are a cinch.

Then back in our room we met the third one of us, called Stevie, who comes from Scotland: I think I shall like her.

Then the adjutant wanted to see us and again we gave the same old particulars. About here it transpired that the actual course doesn't begin till next Monday, why or because of what we're here a week too early we wouldn't know. We're to spend the week making ourselves generally useful in the photographic rooms, hoping to absorb knowledge to help us pass our course whose record hitherto has been a sad series of failures. Between us

124

we've come with a formidable collection of textbooks and intend to spend next week's evenings swotting up as much gen[1] as we think we can.

When they were through showing us around we had supper, visited the NAAFI[2] and came back to our room, swept and cleaned it out, scrounging ruthlessly and illegally for various fittings to make it a little more home-like and that done, we all three of us are now in bed.

15 May 1941

Tuesday wasn't so good. I had an attack of the lostness and 'unbelongingness' I had so badly in the early days in the WAAF – a blow to my concept of my sophistication and self-assurance.

By Wednesday though it was gone. First days in new places anyway are always the worst, so now if not ecstatically happy, I am contented enough and like the work sufficiently well to (I hope) pass the course.

I am beginning to get to know Helga and Stevie better. We got quite matey tonight, showing each other photographs of our respective families and friends in an interlude between washing our underclothing with face soap and tepid water in a minute basin and ironing it afterwards with an iron the size of a postage stamp borrowed from an airman.

I find Helga not so dull as I first suspected, and Stevie

[1] RAF slang for general information.
[2] General shop for the use of Forces personnel.

not so interesting. Both of them make pleasant acquaint-ances, neither bosom friends, we should get on well enough.

We took the station bus in to Marlow last night to see a Western film at the one cinema, walking three miles back, and tonight Stevie and I strolled for an hour through an enchanting wood which had bluebells, primroses and violets.

I've got the day off on Saturday and am going over on Friday night to stay with the Cunninghams and shall make a beeline for their bathroom and by that time they won't want to stop me – and on Monday our course begins.

18 May 1941

I've had a very enjoyable weekend.

On Friday afternoon they told us we could have both Saturday and Sunday off so there followed a frenzied rush to secure the necessary passes and ration cards.

Back in my bedroom I considered my one largish suitcase with disfavour, then I remembered an illegal inspiration of Joyce's, removed my gas mask from my haversack and packed my weekend necessities most suc-cessfully into its various compartments: I should think it's one of the most heinous Air Force sins!

I got a lift by the RAF to Marlow, took the bus with a slight resentfulness – the Services have come to regard any vehicle on any road as part of their transport system – into High Wycombe, from there got a lift into Amer-sham by a woman going to collect her husband. I don't think she was frantically eager to take me, she was in a hurry, but the civilian population has been well trained now into being nice to us. I had to finish the journey from Amersham to Chesham by bus but the whole thing done in just over an hour was pretty satisfactory going.

I still can't get over the niceness of the Cunninghams. If I were really related to them they couldn't have been nicer. They washed and starched to a perfection it's never seen at my hands, my dirty shirt for me. They let me have baths whenever I wanted them. They cleaned my shoes; they brought me early morning tea; they fed me at minute intervals with colossal, heavenly food and in between receiving all this pampering Patsy and I went for walks, to the cinema and talked. Patsy is pretty het up about Stu,[3] he presumably left Canada nearly three weeks ago and hasn't been heard of since. As she's called the wedding banns and bought a super spring trousseau, which is rapidly becoming seasonably unsuitable, her anxiety can be sympathised with.

I also got my hair done and composed a poem to include the wingspans of all the German aircraft, now I'm trying to learn it.

I got back here at about eight this evening, as Patsy and Mrs Cunningham gave me a lift to Wycombe, but had to return early to cope with the putting to bed of evacuees, so I washed and mended and cleaned and

---

[3] Stuart Barrie, who married Patsy soon after and died later in the war.

hairbrushed and generally did what I could to make myself neat and presentable.

Tomorrow five more females arrive to take the course, it seems very unfair that we've had a week of extra preparation. It appears now it won't begin till Tuesday.

19 May 1941

Life is very good right now. We move today from our bleak, bare garret over the stables into the main house. As five more WAAF course takers were expected, they cleared out one of the wings for us and into its end bedroom Stevie, Helga and Joan (now all very chummy) moved after tea. A heavenly angel of a sergeant and his minions helped us.

In our room, which has latticed windows, window seats and a super view through an arched courtyard of the castle grounds, are the only three officers' beds which are large and have mattresses, while the second bedroom – which has to house all five of the new arrivals – has only the iron and narrow and the three biscuits kind.[4] Also our room is so peppered with rugs that only slim slits of the underneath lino show. We've gathered wild flowers from out of bounds boughs and we've tacked onto the walls the cream of our families: Helga is an Honourable and has her ancestral home, Stevie has lots

---

[4] It took three 'biscuit mattresses' – square and flat – to make up a bed.

of horses – still, I have got Cousin John as a sergeant air gunner![5]

Our table is stacked with an imposing pile of books, which we some time hope to read, with Italian and German aircraft sheets tacked above, which we some time hope to study. The whole thing is definitely a very good show, the room rather like the quarters of a college girl, the castle adding to the effect, and we began our course today.

We left the Ops Room and went up into the training wing where we sat in classrooms and studied diagrams on the blackboard, so that it was like being back at school again. All of us discovered unhappily that we had to know how to divide and multiply decimals and all of us had forgotten how, so I spent the morning getting the knowledge again and a headache – I'm not very good at maths.

In the afternoon we met some of the men taking the course – very dim, very uninteresting RAF officers. A stocky, ugly flight lieutenant is taking the course. Report had it that he was somewhat of a stinker, still he looks intelligent, which I cannot say for any other of his pupils.

We had our first lecture after lunch, with the five new WAAFs still not arrived. It was very complicated; I'll have to work very hard. I've got a book on maps and I'm away to it now. Oh yes, and it's a three- not a two-week course so we'll be here a month.

[5] One of the most dangerous jobs of all. An air gunner sat in the back of the aircraft looking for enemy aircraft behind, above and below.

23 May 1941

A WAAF staff officer from Bomber Command is coming to inspect the WAAF detachment here tomorrow so we've been cleaning our room. Three wildly unexciting things remain for me to do – eat my supper, have a bath and do some work.

The course since Monday has trundled on with casualness and haphazardness. Concentrated effort begins next Monday, at least that's somebody's story, but we've heard so many rumours since we've been here we disregard all prophecy and accept only the hour.

Some of the course I like, some I don't. I still don't know whether I want to pass, whether I'm going to like being an officer, but I don't want to go back to Hendon. Molly's gone now, with a posting to a fighter operations station and Boomps has applied for a posting. I don't particularly relish spending the rest of my youth peering down the end of a stereoscope and reading up German industrial, political and economic conditions for relaxation. I've realised already the futility of fighting: life goes on impervious and one has to go with it. I expect, somehow, some time again, I'll have fun.

5 June 1941

Today has been interesting. We had a lecture this morning – not the dull technical ones we've been overpowered with lately about factories and guns and how they work – but on comparisons of the related strengths of the various modern Navies and about the French Air Force and the French attitude generally in the first year of war, a lot of which was revealing as well as instructive. Do you know how the French retaliated on the German daylight raid on Paris, which incidentally agents had warned them about in detail before and about which they did nil? The Germans sent a force of some 300 bombers and the French, in a reprisal raid which headlined all our papers, sent one obsolete bomber which dropped a few ineffectual bombs on a Berlin suburb.

This afternoon we packed into two cars, I unfortunately with Madam Pipont: a civilian female taking the course with us, apparently the Queen of the Admiralty, who *will* call us three 'the children'. It makes Helga the most mad – she's thirty. We drove over to an RAF station where we were assembled and shown flyable models of German aircraft. First we were shown both British and German cameras used in aerial photography, and then we drove across the aerodrome to examine JU88, the ME109 and an ME110 and lastly to see a large part of HE111 in one of the hangars. The man who took us round told us lots about them, like how our people are still trying to find out why it is that German planes can fly at such colossal altitudes, and we climbed up the 110 and looked into the cockpit. Also the place was littered with all sorts of weird types of our own aircraft, including Boeings and Stirlings and Liberators: types I hadn't seen before.

Tomorrow we're going to another aerodrome, Benson, where I believe we might get the chance of a flight. I daren't hope much on the prospect. All these months I've tried vainly to fly and so often I've nearly wangled it and then been disappointed. Incidentally, we've high hopes that we've passed our course, I got back the report I did with 'good' on it and we've been told we can take a week's leave from Saturday, which they'd hardly bother about if we'd failed, we'd just be returned immediately to our units. I think I'll spend it with Joyce getting my uniform and visiting people. I also want to go back to Hendon and collect some more of my luggage.

6 June 1941

I've done it! After all these months: it's happened. I've flown. But I must begin at the beginning and tell you fully how.

We drove over to the aerodome after lunch, I again unfortunately with that infuriating Mrs Pipont. But that to some degree offset by my companion who proved to be very interesting, having escaped from Casablanca after the collapse of France by smuggling himself into a Portuguese freighter and landing in England shoeless and moneyless with only a bundle of shirts.

At the drome we saw first where the films were developed. After, went round an enormous hangar examining various types of aircraft. Then someone suggested that we'd all like a flip. Our guide said it might be arranged for the men anyway, with an unenthusiastic glance at Mrs Pipont. I seethed inwardly with rage at my sex and the general rawness of the deal we were getting. I thought, 'I'll die if they leave me on the ground after all this time I've been in the RAF, having to watch these civilians in uniform being able to go up' – but I didn't have to. Over at Dispersal the pilots raised no objections: we could all go up. A tall, fair, good-looking Canadian pilot officer with a parachute slung over his shoulder said to me, 'Are you going to fly?'

'Yes, if I may.'

'Good show,' and Helga and I walked across the mud-caked grass to the waiting Blenheim.

Service aircraft aren't designed to accommodate females, you have to clamber into them by a series of footholds, sheer on the side and too far apart for a skirt. However, desire overcame all obstacles and in the end we got in, I sitting in the nose and Helga beside the pilot. There was a lot of testing and false starting but at last the roar of the engines increased in volume and we were moving across the drome, our speed increased. The noise was enormous, we were airborne. I looked at the earth a long way beneath me, with only the floor of the plane between that and me, and thought how safe it was with your feet on the ground and through the window I saw the second Blenheim. It appeared motionless, hovering: uncanny and almost terrifying. The only sensation of speed you get is in the actual taking off and in the landing. In the air I cannot believe we were doing 200 mph.

Our nice pilot had asked where we wanted to go and we said to Medmenham, so soon we were weaving around the castle. You couldn't call it a pukka beat-up[6] but he

---

[6] RAF slang for a hair-raising ride full of stunts and speed.

was an excellent pilot, taking us like we were a busload of babies. But there was one bewildering moment, when the earth was up in the sky and the sky down under where the earth ought to have been and God alone knows what had happened to my stomach. It was the sort of sensation that you're a bit frightened about but want to keep on going.

Flying back I got quite blasé and looked down on the tiny remote earth thinking it would be fun if I had some bombs – the destructive instinct ever strong in man is accentuated in the sky when the ground is a thing imper-sonal and detached with no link about it to you.

As we landed, speed rushed up to meet us and with the uprush of the earth, we roared over the grass, bumping and bucking like a ship at sea, to taxi gracefully and finally to Dispersal.

Reluctantly I climbed out and stood with Helga and Stevie by the Dispersal hut waiting for the rest of the party to land.

8 June 1941

The last three days have been chaotic. Saturday was the last day of our course and in the afternoon was our oral examination. I said to myself, 'Well, even if I failed I've flown,' but even the memories of that paradisiacal snicket failed to ease the sickness in my stomach. I thought, 'I can't go back to Hendon and have to march in to work again and everyone know I've failed. And Molly's gone now and probably Boompsie's going. I've gone beyond Hendon. I can't return.'

The exam was to begin at two. At ten past two our waiting jests had an hysterical ring. By half past two we were silent, laughterless, scared. At about twenty to three it started.

I needn't have been so apprehensive; it wasn't anything like as bad as I'd feared. I could answer about 75 per cent of the questions and after tea we were told all three of us were through and that the examiner had been quite impressed with our flow of knowledge.

Then in the next hour we rejoiced, collected chits[7] to say we could buy officer's uniform, collected ration cards, got the address of our new billet, tracked down our passes which the Orderly Room lose for us with monotonous regularity, packed and put ourselves into the Dispersal car, town-bound.

At Joyce's flat there was no Joyce but a letter saying she was on her way back, she hoped, from Southampton, and would I please cope with the squadron leader and hold on to him till she returned.

I'd just read the note when he phoned. I chatted as if we had been chums for years and had him coming round by nine o'clock.

While I was washing away some of the Marlow mud, Joyce returned and after came the squadron leader and a flying officer who bought us drinks and took us to a hotel where we ate and danced and had an amusing evening.

[7] Forms.

We got in about two and annoyingly I woke again at seven and couldn't go back to sleep.

After lunch I went back to the garage with Joyce to accomplish the lengthy business of persuading her sergeant to let her leave early. Everyone congratulated me on my course: only one other girl from Hendon has ever got through.

When we did escape we went to the pictures and came back here, meaning to go to bed early, but instead sat and talked about how both of us had altered since the time we first met and how peculiar a thing was love.

I've taken a flat here for a week and today I've been measured for my uniform. I've spent far too much on sundry odds and ends and the madness always gets me if I put me and money together in a shop.

15 June 1941

So the hectic week has ended. A pleasant week lolling in bed till just when I felt like it with breakfast of coffee and rolls and toast sent up to me in it. Going round town and spending much too much money with occasional pain at the mess in the side streets of London, though it has to be a pretty big ruin these days to make it register. Having fittings for my uniform, drinking beer with Joyce and an architect now in the Army called Ralph, and discussing life deep into the morning.

Walking away from a tailor's in my uniform and accepting my first salute there wasn't the excitement I had expected. Driving with Joyce in her only-just-working motor car down to Dulwich with the luggage we were moving from her flat, and driving back the next morning at even greater speed, knowing that we shouldn't be in town till one, and Stevie and Helga would be waiting since eleven. We met, apologised, ate and piled Stevie, Helga and lots of luggage back into the car and drove to Medmenham. There our commissions, we were told, were effective from 7 July; we have still the masses of inevitable Air Force forms to fill in about them.

Then we were taken to our billets. Stevie and I are billeted together in a doctor's house in Marlow. We have a nice but small room, a sitting room and use of a colossal garden. We can only have one bath a week because there is something the matter with the cesspool. The doctor we don't like, he seems fussy and finicky and interfering.

Today we started working. I got depressed at first, it was strange and I hated the sensation of very newness. My hair wouldn't go right so I felt a mess, which is fatal. We had to wear airwomen's uniform until tomorrow because of another inevitable muddle so we felt awkward and embarrassed in the Officers Mess and again I hate being new anywhere.

By the evening it was better. We'd had a lovely hour lying on our stomachs in the heavenly gardens now open to us, watching goldfish in a pond with one of the officers on our course chatting to us, and at supper a lot of the officers we had taken the course with were there greeting us like old chums. I expect after a while I'll very much like it but it's a jolt after Hendon, where I knew everyone and was one of the eldest, to here where I'm so very raw.

20 June 1941

It's so hot it defies description. Stevie and I, in a minimum of clothing to still be decent, are sweltering in the doctor's sun parlour. He and his hag of a housekeeper are enthroned on the lawn. We don't sit much in the garden here, they almost come round after us shaking up the blades of grass where we've sat.

Walking to Danesfield this morning in a uniform so wickedly hot, I thought as we turned the corner – 'Behold, the flourishing village of Medmenham'. It has a Dog and Badger and a post office cum general store, which pre-war sold everything and now sells nothing, and that's absolutely all. Four miles away, to get to which you have to walk, is the town of Marlow, a little better. These, with Danesfield, constitute my gay surroundings.

I had just got into Third Phase[8] this morning when a Hart appeared in the sky and proceeded to give me the most brilliant exhibition of stunt flying I've yet seen. It dived to within inches of the earth, it rolled, soared, zoomed, twisted, looped the loop, had generally colossal fun, taunting me with my seemingly perpetual exile from people with wings. However, after, I went to look for a town on a map and found three called

---

[8] There were three main stages in Photographic Interpretation – First, Second and Third Phase. Each used a team specialising in different aspects of the work. These included looking for any new developments in fortifications, in movement of troops, of shipping, aircraft or any other new enemy development.

Vogle, Bogle and Erp, which cheered me up considerably.

Lunchtime I had a letter from Molly. I read it in the ante-room and in the second line was the news that Boomps is now a corporal. I just had to shout out about it; Stevie shushed me violently and people looked up from their papers and frowned. That's the biggest thing that's so unbearable, that and the fact that after we've finished work there's nothing to do. Stevie and I did bathe in the river one evening, getting out of our costumes and into slacks and shirts only, hoping our part of the field was deserted, but mostly we sit and listen to the radio and I write letters or this diary or read *Maud*, a really entrancing book I've discovered. What I long to do now is to go on just one almighty binge and laugh and shout and shriek so I get it all out of me.

And the men here! I can't even be bothered to talk to the majority of them; I can't think of anything to say. With the fighter crowd I always knew and just had to laugh and shoot a line. If I stay here I'll just be a cabbage, a Medmenham cabbage, the most deadly dull of all varieties. For the first time since it began I am looking forward now to the end of the war. I'm sorry this has been such a moan, I'm sorry I'm such a worthless person, not finding full bliss in the knowledge that I am at last really helping towards the war effort.

21 June 1941

I am sorry about yesterday, it was one of those regrettable lapses I am still apt to retreat to in my weaker hours.

I am feeling saner now so maybe the letting it out has helped some.

They gave me my first sortie[9] today to do on my own which I liked doing tremendously, especially as neither Helga nor Stevie has progressed yet from practice sorties and filing (which I detest). And after I'd finished it Mr Wavel, in charge of Third Phase, said, 'Let me congratulate you, Miss Bawden, on your first original effort,' which made me feel very, very smooth.

I'll try and show you Third Phase: a large, one sided windowed room, with its sloping desks, high stools, desk lamps and general litter, maps, photographs, files, stereoscopes, rulers, dividers and other individually cherished devices to simplify effort. At each of the desks sits a WAAF officer with jacket off and shirtsleeves rolled to the elbow (because it's hot). There's Robbie[10] who seems cheery and helpful and pleasant, with the oddest accent which appears at unexpected intervals. There's Tommy, who's tall and dark and attractive without any make-up, because I watched her once with deepest envy wash her face and dry it off looking just the same. Then there's

[9] The photographic sorties over enemy territory in Europe were flown from nearby RAF Benson. An experienced interpreter stationed at Benson viewed the newly developed sortie, sending the photographs and his report on to the Photographic Interpretation Unit (PRU) at RAF Medmenham for further and fuller interpretation.

[10] Shea Robinson.

Babs,[11] who does aircraft, and lots more of them but they'll have to wait for another time when I feel like it, along with the personalities of Second Phase.

22 June 1941

I'm lying on the bed in my bathing costume waiting for Helga to call for me to go for a bathe. It continues to be so hot as to make us loathe the heaviness of our uniforms. There was quite a stir at breakfast this morning as Germany has marched into Russia. Really, this war. Events get so fantastic that I've given up trying to follow it sanely and normally. I think most other people are getting the same way about it. Mostly at table they joked about it, a few people made estimates on the Front Line comparisons of German and Russian Armies and Air Forces. One wag offered bets on the length of time before the Russian government arrived in England. The general prediction was that Germany would be across that country in a matter of weeks (interlude here while Helga called and we went for our bathe. The water was heavenly but a tragedy occurred. I hate the feel of the reeds wrapping round my legs and, kicking violently free from them, lost one of Stevie's bathing shoes I'd borrowed and also had to limp painfully back one shoe less and sore).

[11] Constance Babington Smith (1912–2000), author and wartime photographic interpreter who made the first identification from a photograph of a German V1 flying bomb at Peenemunde (1943). In 1945 she was awarded an MBE.

I suppose now the Russians are our allies, personally I hate the idea. I think the Russians are a lot of scum, every bit as much a menace to peaceful progress as the Germans. Besides, look at the way they attacked Finland and snatched their share of Poland: I certainly don't blame the Finns for joining the Germans against the Russians. How bitterly and unforgivably they must hate the Russians and with what just cause. At least with the Germans they have a sporting chance of vengeance; with us they have only our utterly ineffective moral support. How can we fight with such slugs as the Russians against such heroes as the Finns? If I were a British soldier I would refuse to fight against Finnish troops, I couldn't do it. I think the best idea would be to leave the filthy Russians and the foul Germans to fight it out, and even better to add to the lot the unmentionable Japs, for years and years and years in the middle of some Russian plain, so that the rest of the world could get on with normal living and so that they don't stop fighting until all are dead. Seriously, though, I do think it a good idea to have these enemies of progress fighting each other. How happy it makes me to think that right now, every minute, there are a few less Germans and Russians in existence. Rearm as hard as we can, but join with the Russians? Never, never, never. Talk about trying to buddy up with a tiger!

24 June 1941

I had a day's leave yesterday. I felt fine leaving the house and knowing that the day was my own and I hadn't any work at all to do in it. For the first part down the road to Medmenham, a squadron leader and a flying officer gave me a lift in their car. I haven't felt I could consider the squadron leader a buddy of mine ever since cold words were exchanged when I was still a corporal, as to whether I had any right to be in the main hall. However, he was for him quite pleasant in the car and I treated him a little less frostily myself.

After they left me, there were still the three miles to the station. Officers shouldn't hitch-hike, so I walked sedately for about 100 yards and then a hay lorry passed me. No one was around so I did my stuff. As a result I had a terrific ride to town resulting in my catching an earlier train than I had hoped.

I was going over to Hendon, partly to collect the final block of my belongings and partly to see Boomps. But Boomps had gone, she'd left three days earlier, to go to Oxford to train for her code and cipher commission. I am so pleased about it for her, she hated Hendon without Molly and me. And she does her discipline training at Gerrards Cross, so I'll be able to see her plenty.

So I had lunch instead with Freda, got my hair done, bought myself the snappiest sunsuit for 5s 11d, which I am wearing now in the doctor's garden, what there is of it, and then went over to Hendon.

They welcomed me back like a queen – airmen, WAAFs, the wardens at the gate, all saluted me – and I could hardly walk a yard without someone stopping to congratulate and chat to me.

One of the defence officers, a Pilot Officer Kelly, took

143

me down to the Officers Mess to tea, and crowds of the officers I had known came in to talk to me. I can't describe how glad I was to be back again.

Afterwards I went down to where the WAAF officers live to call on Mrs Wright. While waiting for her I lolled in the garden, drinking gin and lime after gin and lime and telling the other officers about my course.

Then Mrs Wright arrived and I stayed to dinner. We talked for about an hour after and I told her how dull I was so far finding Medmenham existence. She said, 'I can't imagine you, Bawden, staying dull for long in any place,' which cheered me up. And we talked about the fun we had had in the past and retold some of the riper Hendon scandals. She said one thing that still makes me chuckle. 'I'll always remember you and Riley [Molly] at dances, surrounded by crowds of alluring officers and looking incredibly demure.'

At nine I had to fly to catch the last train back to this centre of existence and by dint of a great deal of charm and pathos on the MT driver at the garage, I got an illegal lift back to my billet in the same famous motorcycle that first brought me here. Altogether a delightful day.

I got up this morning feeling terrific. I thought – I still have fun, I won't be a cabbage. Then at the door the doctor was waiting for me, to moan endlessly and unpleasantly about how I'd banged the door last night. With that and the knowledge that I was walking down the road to work and there was no escape and no return ever for me, I stayed soaked in misery most of the morning, until I went up and moaned for some minutes to The

Tortoise.[12] I don't think, though, that I am ever going to like any of the WAAF officers here the way I liked my friends at Hendon; they're an odd collection. I am the sort of person people either like very much or dislike with equal intensity, there are rarely half measures. I suppose having had a long turn of the kind of people who like me I am due for the sort who most definitely don't.

29 June 1941

I remember Molly saying to me that last Saturday I saw her, 'The funny thing is that I don't seem to mind about anything any more. When they told me to move my room for the third time I just did what they told me and I remember being surprised that I was doing it and not minding.'

Walking back here tonight with David Brackey, the interpreter from Shipping section, I thought, 'It's getting like that with me now.' I found out pretty definitely today that I shan't be going into Camouflage[13] after all, but I didn't much care. I found I was too apathetic to attempt any protesting or counter-action. I just accept the things now that happen to me without regret or protest. So I try not to think about anything, just accept each unpleasant day as it comes, keep on telling myself that I should be

---

[12] A fellow interpreter, so called due to the fact he looked like one! (I.e. small and bald.)

[13] The Camouflage section was in charge of studying photographs for German disguises of planes or aerodromes or weapons.

glad that at last I am doing something worthwhile and try to stop myself from indulging in memories of my past months.

Tonight, I went into Stevie's room. Stevie is a girl who believes in telling the painful truth. During the last few days I have learnt – with incredulity, bewilderment and distress – the news from her that: (a) I am intolerably noisy and bang doors to such an extent that people in Second Phase see my approach with apprehensive moans, (b) I am loathed and detested by the doctor and his house-keeper hag. The second really did shake me. I'd been happily of the assumption that I had been particularly considerate and thoughtful during my forced residence in their hateful house. Instead, apparently the noise of my passage through it is reducing their endurance to shreds. With Stevie they allow use of phone, use of room to iron in, use of extra cupboards, but nothing most definitely to me, except a deep desire to see my departure (which I am effecting with every possible haste).

2 July 1941

So I thought it was pretty dumb to stay both in a job and a billet I dislike and one, anyway, was redeemable. I took myself firmly in hand, told myself I had more guts surely than to be so abjectly defeated by an atmosphere, and went along with Stevie billet-hunting in Marlow. Marlow, at least, represents a little more civilisation: it has shops, a cinema, a station and a swimming club.

After a series of failures we came to a high wooden

gate. I liked the look of it so we went inside, walking up a pretty garden to a white square house. The front and back doors were open and also most of the windows, but no one was in. I liked most tremendously the look of the place. I'll skip the details, I think they'd be tedious for the next hour. The climax of which found Stevie fixed to live with a family up the road and I am in the house. Two elderly ladies own it, but nice elderly people, kind people, not stinkers like our present billet. I am going to like my bedroom; I have a large double bed and a large room with a desk in it. I'll try to get my typewriter out of store and I'll like that, having time and opportunity to write again.

The war may well go on for years and years and I don't think, however much I keep on to myself about it, that I'll be able to raise enough patriotism and sense of duty to resign myself with any contentment to life at Marlow.

We had a lecture on our course about being aware of the pomposity of experts. People here should listen to that, never in my life have I met such a self-satisfied, smug, limited, visionless sort of person as there are at RAF Medmenham. I'll grant them that they are doing valuable work but other people too are doing work of equal value. They make such gods of each other, the three flight lieutenants here; you almost need trumpeters to precede their passage and chanting choirs singing, 'Behold they come, Holy of Holies'.

11 July 1941

Life lately has been a rush of almost the proportions of my Hendon days, with lots of things happening, the way I like it, only some of them unpleasant and not so much to my delight.

It began with my riding pillion on a motorcycle from Medmenham to Marlow. For the first time in my life, racing down the road at enormous speed and my thinking, 'oh gosh, this is terrific fun,' to discover later that I had flouted about the most stringent rule of RAF officers in doing so.

Then there was a tragedy, when my future billet's evacuee got measles and I couldn't go in (it seems I am haunted by measles) and had to pelt unsteadily down to Marlow one lunch hour on a borrowed bicycle to find accommodation in a nearby cottage, resulting in an unbelievably relaxing week of tea in bed and all my washing done for me and general willingness, so that, but for the prospect of a bath, a bigger room and an inside WC, I'd be upset at going.

And then there have been the evenings when I've swum from the Marlow Rowing Club and sat after getting more freckles and no more tan on the grass on the river bank. And the day I had off where a flying officer here drove me in his ancient Lanchester over to Oxford where I met Joyce and Boomps in the Randolph and talked for hours, and feasted my wings-starved eyes on the sight of endless alluring young pilot officers and sergeant pilots. And driving back at night, blessedly cool after the heat of the day, with a welcome wind blowing in our faces and an enormous yellow moon in the sky, for once the silhouette of a Wellington with its navigation lights on. The flying officer who drove was small and plain and without any attraction for me and I remembered achingly in the foolish way one aches unguarded in the night, another drive in another night in winter, without such a setting, sitting silent, contented, willing time to cease passing and make our moment together eternal.

The next day I went down to Ipswich to see Molly. She was waiting there on the platform, looking so brown, so well, so happy. We were so excited at seeing each other, we ran to meet, laughing, down the platform. We had lunch and tea together and we walked and talked and made hopeful, probably impossible plans, of getting together and having fun like we used to have.

Too soon I had to come back here, with only a fleeting glance at Ipswich, but with plans of her coming here next Thursday week and my going there on my August forty-eight hours.

The day after was inevitably unpleasant. Flight Lieutenant Stephenson had Helga and me out and told us that they were of the opinion that we were neither of us temperamentally suited to the work and we didn't seem to have the right outlook about it. The right outlook, he explained, seemed to consist of working late every night, giving up one's days off and working on them. In short, just working with time off to eat and sleep and nothing else for the duration. He more or less indicated that we would probably be asked later to take another type of commission. He said they wanted the researching, patient type person; I am neither. Also I detest the civilian in charge of our section and because I won't toady, he detests me. And I don't think the work is the only thing in my whole life or the only thing in the war. So I went back to my work and thought about it.

I decided I'd stick it out while they needed me, even though I was unhappy because it was the war and it was my duty. But if they don't want me then I have done my bit and I can go back to where I belong with an easy conscience. To that end, yesterday evening was spent drinking beer in the Chequers and later swimming with Joyce and an alluring boyfriend just acquired and a sergeant here I know; now I must go and wash and get to bed.

16 July 1941

Since I've written last in this I have had forty-eight hours' leave and spent them with Mother who was spending the week in town. Mother was so very pleased to be back again, she hates it so much being domesticated outside Liverpool. She belongs as a businesswoman in the West End. We saw two films and the new Coward show, *Blithe Spirit*, making you hurt: laughing funny. And Ivor Novello was in the Stalls kissing a lot of people. Also we got taken to tea in the Piccadilly hotel and on one of those days had lunch at Claridge's. They've opened a coserie there where you get a plate of hors d'oeuvres and a champagne cocktail plus roll and butter for 5s 6d. You go to a buffet in the middle of the room and help yourself to your hors d'oeuvres. They craftily only supply quite small plates but carefully and with equal cunning I built my collection of hors d'oeuvres upwards to climax with a mound of some inches up in the air, which the chef supervising gave a very dirty look at. I had several minutes of delighted satisfying guzzle; hors d'oeuvres are a passion of mine, and I bet they made no profit out of me.

Mother and I cramped our style after by trying to find the Ladies without asking in the most unsuccessful effort to look like regular habitués and then ending by having to ask and making ourselves and our searchings twice as conspicuous.

And back again here I didn't, surprisingly, find myself in my usual after leave depression. I was helped probably by a letter from Molly. 'It was wonderful seeing you last Wednesday, you looked stunning in that uniform,' and a box of chocs from Joyce in return for the cigarettes I'd been supplying her with and while eating the evening meal my roving eye reported that some of the people on the new course looked almost possible. I chatted at the meal with quite a reasonable-looking soul on the right and when he said he was getting his own car he became ever more charming. Going back to Marlow in the bus I smiled, almost laughed, and thought with shock – why I'm quite liking it here. My zest in living is back, I will have fun, even here I'll have it.

When I said I'd go from here happily I wasn't being entirely honest; I thought I was but I was wrong, my conscience wasn't easy over my arguments. I'd still be to some degree a quitter if I go. And now I'm having a domestic evening in my room with its large square bed, its two lots of windows, its desk and chest and its easy chair and my two dear old Cranford ladies who bring me in tea in the morning in their flannel dressing gowns and nightcaps.

20 July 1941

To go back to yesterday, we heard that Mrs Trefusis Forbes[14] (apparently suddenly aware that there were 30 WAAF officers snugly at Medmenham, none of whom had been on the WAAF officers disciplinary course[15]) was coming down to see what we were like. The general idea was to be so immaculately tidy that when she did see us it was made obvious to her that here were WAAF officers already perfect beyond improvement. They suggested to me that I did something about my hair. I remembered suddenly a previous conversation.

'I hate girls with short hair,' Red said.

'When I want to get rid of you then, I'll know what to do: I'll cut off my hair.'

---

[14] Dame Katherine Trefusis-Forbes was the first director of the Women's Auxiliary Air Force, given the rank Air Chief Commander.

[15] The disciplinary course in Gerrards Cross was where WAAF were supposed to go before Medmenham but due to the urgent need for interpreters we had managed to skip it.

'You'll have to do more than that, Joan, to get rid of me.'

So we all wore our best uniform and took off our nail varnish and hooked up our hair, and then she didn't come but sent a substitute. A wing officer with a lot of polished practice charm graciously condescended to meet us.

At tea today Dorothy Collins, one of the girls in the Press section, asked me how I liked it here. I hedged warily for a while, and then came clean. I said I thought the work would be most tremendously interesting but I loathed the people I work with. She said, 'Come up and see me after tea.' I did and found four more fugitives from the Medmenham hags, others who had raised such hell until they escaped and I thought, 'If they can, so too can I.' One, Mrs Denise Cooper, made me laugh, telling me tales of her early experience in their clutches. And with her, as with me, and as with the others, she was never allowed to do anything but file.

After leaving them I went down to see Corkie, our admin officer. She's a dear and we all like her a lot. I said I wanted to put in an application to leave the unit. She said at once, 'You needn't tell me why, it's those three bitches for whom you work.' She was tremendously kind; she said she'd see the group captain tonight and get something done about it. When people are sorry for me I can never take it; kindness always gets me. She said, 'Go this way, my dear, nobody will ever see you then.' So I stayed for a minute or two in the adjoining empty room pulling myself together.

23 July 1941

Corkie has talked to me, and thanked me for my courage in making my complaint. Lots of others had suffered similarly but none would step forward. I had and she was with me to the death. Then Mrs Hamalrick spoke to me (she's one of the three hags), after people had been coming and going and telephones ringing mysteriously all morning. From her also I learnt, with surprise and suspicion, that I have a great future before me as an interpreter, that she had told Stephenson to talk to me but not like that and it was all a horrible mistake. That if I would only stay and withdraw my application I could have a section of my own, care and attention would be flourished upon me and life would be a long happy song. So I said I'd think about it and I did.

It seemed to me on thinking that with everybody from the CO to Mrs Hamalrick all so petrified that higher powers should hear that anyone could be wanting to leave this precious place (as I mentioned before, it's apparently a terrific honour to be here at all and, according to the rest here, the place at the RAF is reserved only for the brainy select), I pretty well had them by the ears and could get what I wanted out of them. So I said to Mrs Hamalrick I thought it would be much more satisfactory if I asked the CO personally for myself instead of writing out any more applications, upon which she looked extremely sour and tried not to show too obviously that the idea to her simply stank.

Tomorrow I shall present the CO my ultimatum: they

either let me go to Mrs Hemalrick's department (she has a sense of humour) and into the newly formed Middle East section, or I go. A little while ago I'd have gone anyway, another section or no other section, but now, beyond my work life, here isn't so utterly bloody. My battle for my rights has won me many sympathetic acquaintances, it's stopped raining and I've been swimming. For two evenings I've been mildly pub crawling with people from the new course. My billet is all heavenly bliss. Molly's coming tomorrow for the day and that's my news to date, more of the crisis anon.

30 July 1941

For far too many days I have been saying I must have a domestic evening tonight, until the immediate threat of a breakdown in my self-supporting system enforced one tonight. So I've washed endless pairs of stockings, sewed on three buttons, given my shoes and buttons a little more then their usual flick around, contemplated even washing my hair and decided it was time I wrote up my diary before I indulge in the nice things: a bath, a book in bed, some biscuits, milk and some chocolate (my underground chocolate-securing system is a miracle of organisation and ingenuity).

I'll just flick through what has happened. The day on the river in the heavenly sun with Molly and Richard, and Molly staying the night here with me; lying on my stomach at the end of our punt, trailing my fingers in the water while Richard paddled and Molly sat laughing at the other end, brown and unbelievably beautiful, wearing a yellow frilled hat that on anyone else would look like an utterly idiotic cake doily but on her was perfect. And my war which fizzled out in the tame way that wars in life usually do with vague promises of future sweeping reforms and the information that the CO will see me himself in a month's time if I still want to be posted.

Lots of hints of lots of alterations of life at Medmenham. We Third Phase are going onto a shift system; we're to have ten more people and we shall work in three shifts and get some time off (in the day) at last. The recurrent dreadful rumour, that there really is going to be a WAAF hostel for WAAF officers, has started circulating yet again with a fresh and imposing amount of supporting evidence. But something will have to be done here about: (a) the meals when 150 people fight like steers for chairs and food intended for 50, and (b) the morning bus, when thirty-odd officers crush like cattle into a lorry to be jolted and jarred to their place of duty.

A day off on Friday when, if it's fine, I fly. Suddenly I was gay again, suddenly I was laughing and I didn't care and the desolate misery of the past weeks was behind me. I was all those things I thought I would never be again: uncaring, unselfconscious, mad, a little bad and fun. I broke the silence of the ante-room to joke with our American visitors, a USA Fleet Air Arm member, so that everyone was laughing with plans for his return to the States with all the WAAFs here going with him; and at dinner I joked with the younger and almost passable members of the latest course. Now I'm dressing for a dance, the first dance since Hendon – please don't let it be too much of a flop; I want so much to hear music and to dance till I drop.

2 August 1941

Today was terrific fun. I went over to Hendon in the afternoon as Richard[16] had promised to take me flying. He was up when I arrived so I went to see his squadron leader – one of my elderly and useful admirers. He entertained me till Richard's return, showing me over his private plane and being won round to the idea of my having a flip. Then Richard collected me and we went over to the Dispersal hut. The weather was dull so he said we'd better wait a while to see if it got any better. We went into the pilots' room and for half an hour I talked and joked with him and three others of the squadron; there was a map on the wall and books, papers and flying kit on the table and floor. They perched on the backs of their chairs, smoking, talking to me; their tunics were ancient, their wings frayed, they were young, untidy and contented. Then Richard said we'd do a weather test. Someone lent me a flying jacket, another lent me a helmet and showed me how to use the intercom. I couldn't wear a parachute because of my skirt but Richard said it wouldn't matter as we wouldn't be going high enough for me to use it anyway.

[16] Richard was Molly's boyfriend. In the end he married a different WAAF.

They found a stepladder for me to get into the Lysander, it's terribly high off the ground, and Woody buckled me in. Then we were taxiing past SHQ and I thought of all the days I'd sat there seeing planes go by and wishing I were in them and now, incredibly, it was happening; we were taking off, then airborne. I looked down at the aerodrome below me, so neat and clean, small and tidy like one of my aerial photographs, impossible that people lived and worked on it. We went higher, the earth remote, I saw some children playing on a lawn looking like gay darting flags. I couldn't see Richard at all. Once I thought the engine had stopped and I imagined the dreadfulness of this death I would fall to. I decided I'd shut my eyes when it came, but it didn't and I wasn't afraid any more, only contented and wanting it never to stop. I wanted to go terrifically high and terribly fast up to the remoter air where only the Spitfires and Hurricanes go, where the earth isn't visible any more and it's a new world and you a strange new person. But the weather was rotten and we had to come in again pretty soon. When we halted outside the Dispersal hut the doors were thick with airmen to watch my reactions. It's a rare event (at Hendon anyway): a WAAF flying.

After, Richard and I got caught up in a Mess cocktail party with lots of group commanders and other exalted beings until they drove me at great speed to catch my train. A terrific day but it's foul now back here with all those dreary old men.

11 August 1941

A lot of days and a lot of things have passed and happened since I wrote this up last. There was Molly coming here to spend four of her seven days' leave with me, and Richard staying too in Marlow to spend his leave with Molly, and the first evening of it when Tony Robinson came over from Benson in his peculiar car and the four of us went pub crawling. Outside one pub, after a piece of showing off by Tony in the car-backing line, he was deservedly punished by the self-starter refusing to stop. The row was terrific, and seeing as all the works were under my seat, I was ejected from the car. Tony removed the cushion, dropped a spanner into it and showers of sparks and other oddments shot upwards and still the noise continued. I had to hold myself up because my stomach hurt so much with my laughing while Tony, who is not a mechanic, said, 'It's usually a very good car,' and Richard, who used to be an engineer, finally got the noise to stop and quite a lot of the car to work again, enough anyway to get Tony back to Benson.

28 August 1941

A lot has happened since I wrote this up. There was my birthday. Now I'm twenty-two. Looking back: a little sad, in part regretful, in part dazed by the rush of it, but largely satisfied with the events, the colour, the variety and the people that crammed into each hour, extended each day and pushed into wild speed each month so that the year from twenty-one to twenty-two was a swift year, a more vital year than any of the others of my life and I wonder what will happen in the time till I'm twenty-three.

Tony Robinson phoned in the evening and came over to take me out to celebrate our respective one-day-after-each-other's birthdays. Getting ready, I said to myself – you've got to realise that all anyone really has is the present, this time that's passing now. So I decided not to regret that it was only Tony Robinson, whom I've known nearly all the time I was at Hendon and who had been the faithful if unexciting standby of Molly and myself.

I was rewarded with a wonderful evening. It was the first time I had ever really talked to Tony and I found I could talk about anything. We had dinner at Maidenhead, drinks in a pub just outside Marlow and talked all the time about love, marriage, children, things we liked, ways of living. He's a very good type, Tony. He's regular Air Force. He's got a job and a not too badly paid one. He'll move about all the time, will probably go abroad and at the end of the war he wants a farm to retire to. Tony kissed me once lightly goodnight, too quickly for me to know how my senses reacted.

On the Saturday evening I went over to Chesham to stay till Monday morning with Patsy and Biddy. Patsy is married now to Stu and was home while he changed stations. Now guess what squadron he's been posted to: 504. So I was told my first news since Christmas of Red. He'd been sent out of the squadron onto an instructors course. He got to drinking so heavily at Exeter that he became no good as a fighter pilot. Red, exiled from the life he loved, Red no longer the fighter pilot who'd been to France and had shot down five Huns, Red no longer the youngest, the toughest, the gayest of the squadron, I can only pity. The promised pay-off, the catching up of what he certainly had coming, gives me no satisfaction.

On Tuesday I came home on four days' leave, travelling to Liverpool in a First Class sleeper, one of the few being-an-officer advantages. Already here I'm bored, already I want to go back, I've so completely outgrown home. I'm adult now, I'll never go back again.

2 September 1941

At Medmenham so little ever happens I have little occasion to write this up. It was several days ago that I got Patsy's letter telling me that Red was now at Cranwell.[17] For a day I had a renewal of the pain I had endured in the weeks immediately after he'd left me. I thought, 'He's out of the squadron now away from the way of life that separated us and made impossible our togetherness. He's alone, older, if I go to him surely he will want me.' Scenes I thought I had forgotten came crowding back, words we had spoken I remember so that it sometimes seems as if every second of our time together is branded in my brain. I went so far as to look up trains to Cranwell; I sank so low as to draft a letter to bring him to town for a day. I fought my final battle: whether to go back or

[17] The RAF training establishment.

to forget, life with Red or life without him, and then suddenly I was decided, I knew there was no return.

3 September 1941

I had a letter from Joyce today. Johnny Fletcher has been missing since early in August and she's only just found out. Poor, poor Joyce. She loved Johnny very much, he was no good and never would have married her but what a person is makes no difference to how you love them. I'm going down to her station, Duxford, to see her tomorrow. There's so little a person can do but maybe it will help a little to have me there if she wants to cry. I knew Johnny and I was her friend. We had made a muck-up of our living, Joyce and I, which is a pity because we're both nice people, particularly Joyce. The snag in life is that you pay for everything and that we're having the pay-off now for the days last year when we lived on the assumption that we would be dead tomorrow, only I think it's rather tough we should have to suffer – there wasn't any other way we could have lived then.

16 September 1941

There was a memo recently, asking for overseas volunteers, to which all of us Medmenham-haters joyfully added our names and now, when being here gets too beastly, we ease it by planning our future lives in Heliopolis or Singapore.

There was also the exodus of the WAAF officers from

162

Marlow into our Mess at Henley, Phyllis Court, once a luxury tennis club but now bare, barren and bleak, bereft of carpets and all of its comforts and the walls boasting revolting antelope horns. However, I've got a room to myself and, even if it's small and has a view of three grey walls, it does possess a radiator and one of the very few remaining carpets, with a large ink stain in the middle of it. Anyway, with time I expect the place will improve and the food is wizard and the gardens are lovely and there is the feeling that with all this time to myself I must usefully employ it, not waste it in cinemas and pubs and that I should write again. Only these days I am empty of ideas and there is no background against which I can build.

29 September 1941

One day last week I met Joyce in town and we had a day together of shopping and eating and my trying to cheer her up about Johnny, only I cannot say to her the truth: that he was a cad and a heel and only redeemed by the bravery of his death and that he never loved her as she loved him, and that had he lived he never would have married her; that he had humiliated her repeatedly, treated her cruelly and was selfish, impossible and unworthy. She loved him more than I have known anyone to love and went on loving him deeply and unalterably even after he had left her and was living with another woman. Now she says her life is pointless and dead and cold; it seems so revoltingly unfair that someone so unworthy could make a person as kind, as attractive and as genuine as Joyce so miserable.

Joyce that day freed me finally from Red. She told me that she had met someone who knew him and that he had been boasting about me and not only me, but another girl he had been having a flat-out affair with just after. For a little time I was wretched to think that our affair had been nothing but a brief amusement to him. But after I saw what friends, by their conciliatory 'he did love you only he was young and a fighter pilot and he knew it would never work out', had hidden from me: that he never had loved me, never for an instant, as I had loved him. Nothing permanent ever tied us.

2 October 1941

I have remarked before how life has weeks of dreariness with no indication that the future will be in any way altered from this pointless present. Then suddenly, unexpected, unhoped-for events and colour and chaotic hours come crowding out of a hidden tomorrow to make a rich today.

I went on Monday down to Duxford to spend sixty hours' leave with Joyce. The first part was fine if uneventful, spent talking about Johnny and trying to console her, meeting Joyce's co-WAAF officers (pleasant enough people if not striking individuals), playing set after set of satisfactory tennis and hanging out of Joyce's bedroom window to watch a Hurricane squadron stunting against a green and yellow sunset.

Then in the evening we went to a party in the Officers Mess: Joyce and I and two plainish WAAF officers. I stood about half an hour of being a lady and being content with the one bold squadron leader buying us drinks, and then my lust for living and excitement, which pops up always at parties, cast a look round the pilots in the room and decided, 'Come on, Joan, this is where you go out on your own.'

Then I saw O'Leary who was a bad type who used to be at Hendon, so I went up to him and said hello and he remembered me and we took up from where we had left there, some six months ago. He was slightly drunk and moody and bitter and jealous. If I danced with anyone else he behaved abominably, which I tolerated only because of his promise to take me flying early the next morning. Still, the evening was exciting and flecked with danger and that, after Medmenham, was always welcome. And I coped by being equally rude and unrousably indifferent with the moods of O'Leary who, when he did dance, danced like a dream.

O'Leary apparently married a woman because she said she was having his baby, only to be told after the wedding she was glad some sucker had fallen for that story at last, upon which he apparently tried to shoot her and has never seen her since, so, if true, there is some excuse for his moodiness but he is still a bad type. By being outrageously rude I made him angry enough not to come all the way home with me, thus avoiding the inevitable parting clinch. I am through with all that now; except briefly excited at parties, it is never what I want.

At 8.30 the next morning I met O'Leary at the aerodrome gates and walked out with him to his squadron Dispersal. There, with the help of a flight sergeant and sergeant pilot, I put on overalls, flying jacket, helmet and gloves and the four of us walked over to the Manchester, the first two amusing themselves with libellous statements on the flying career of O'Leary in whose hands, according to them, my death was inevitable. Then followed the now familiar routine of putting on my parachute, being belted into my seat and our taxiing across the landing field with the promise that he was going to stunt and that, no matter what he did and what I thought about it, I was not to touch the stick of the dual control.

We took off, Maggie was a slow little plane: it seemed to move slowly in the air and give a feeling of suspension and security. Then he put down her nose and dived and threw her generally about in the air, then he grinned back at me and said we would loop the loop. I saw his head and the nose of the plane going up over me and for a muddled few moments I was pressed down to pulp and then pushed out to elongated length with the sky disappearing below and the earth coming up to take its place above us. Then I shut my eyes and wondered with a curious absence of emotion whether I should faint. I didn't, nor even felt the least bit sick and was mad at myself for shutting my eyes. However, later he did it again twice running and this time I watched it more detachedly. It appears as if you never move at all but the earth and sky circle around you and the most odd things happen to your stomach.

Joyce was waiting for me and, having rejected an offer of a lift to London in an ambulance along with a couple of corpses, we drove into Cambridge where we looked at books and I bought two prints to brighten my room. Then we caught the train, which got in early enough to town so that we could see Charles Boyer in *Hold Back the Dawn*, before I caught my Medmenham train.

In the evening, going onto night duty, there were five more letters for me. One was from Patsy telling me that Norman Hunt had been killed. It was a year ago now, those fantastic brief days when I knew him. How can he be blamed for his cramming into his twenty years all the sensation he could get because, as he said himself then, he wasn't living long. First John Gurteen, now Norman, two I'd known well, dead, in addition to the uncounted casual acquaintances. Poor Norman, he was a no-good type but what else could he have been and he played pretty straight with me.

16 October 1941

Last night Tony came over. It was to have been his farewell visit before his posting on detachment, only now he isn't going until the 27th. We went to the Catherine Wheel and the Angel, and I chose to drink whisky, which wasn't very wise. I found I was proud of Tony, practically the only person there with wings and only twenty-one and a flying officer and he is to be a flight lieutenant at Christmas.

This morning he came over at half past nine. He had

to go over to Hendon to a Court of Inquiry, over an airman he had minced up slightly with his propeller, and took me too. It was a lovely early autumn morning with the leaves just turning and falling. He brought an air map with him and we plotted our way as we went, it was terrific fun.

At Hendon he went off to his Inquiry and I to see Freda and Connie and Mrs Wright, with whom I went into Golders Green to lunch.

At just after two Tony was ready and we started back. I was feeling a bit low; McCloud is dead now. McCloud who married Margaret Jennings only about a year ago. I saw them both last time I was at Hendon at that cocktail party. They were so gay and so young, it's just hell. And then going past Northolt, we saw the sight that no one can see unaffected, a wing of Spitfires taking off, flying up into the sky. We knew the way better and we talked.

Tony at last does talk a lot to me now. He has his future life so beautifully taped. He's going to get the DFC[18] and be a flight lieutenant and then he's coming off Ops and taking a less spectacular and safer job. The job he's in now is one of the ace flying jobs of the war, and if you're alive when you've done your share of it you can get almost anything. Then after the war he's doing his overseas service, going to India to shoot tigers or whatever they do there to them. And he's getting married and going with his wife and children and dogs

[18] Distinguished Flying Cross.

from RAF station to RAF station. He's regular Air Force so he can. And then he's retiring and buying a farm and pottering in that till he dies: sounds a pretty perfect life.

4 December 1941

I have neglected this for a lot of days. I've told nothing about my week's leave, my re-seeing of Mother back at her Cheltenham job and my staying with her in a room next to hers. She hated it so much: living without a job in Liverpool with relations-in-law. She is the fashion supervisor now of Cavendish House and enjoying living again. I have the most tremendous admiration and respect for my mother as a person; for her courage, her honesty and her kindness, besides my feelings for her as a mother. She gave me my breakfast in bed; we went to the pictures; I had two farewell evenings with the Cunninghams' Peter on embarkation leave for Burma.

Neither have I told you anything about my Air Ministry interview for posting to the Middle East. We volunteered for overseas service some months ago, suffered our inoculations and then were told it was most unlikely we would ever be wanted.

Then the resigned uneventfulness of our Medmenham life was shattered by an Air Ministry summons for twelve of us. The six I was with left early in the morning. We had an enormous and satisfying breakfast at the Paddington Hotel and then went on to Ariel House. Joyce met me there, we had arranged before to spend the day together in town. I passed the Board, I passed the medical.

I rejoined Joyce to eat and see a film, with the unbeliev-able incredible knowledge that in the course of weeks I would be on my way to the Middle East.

Back here it has been even more impossible. There is an occasional reminder in the way of a new rumour or a letter from Air Ministry about tropical kit, bringing the realisation that any day now may be the day when it comes. I hope so much we go all round Africa the way the last lot went and see Sierra Leone, Cape Town and Durban. I can't believe it really will happen to me, to be able to travel at last: the one thing that I really want to do.

8 December 1941

On Saturday at lunchtime, Robbie came into the dining room where we were having an argument with one of our Americans about the respective strengths of the British and American Navies. Robbie said the adjutant wanted to see the seven of us about something connected with our overseas posting, so I bolted my chocolate pudding and left the arguers to it.

None of us was prepared for what he told us: that we were to go that day on embarkation leave. It certainly did shake us. Then followed hours of chaos. No one knew anything – what we should take, what we should do. Everyone except the adjutant was on leave and he was preparing to go.

Anyway, they gave us ration cards and warrants and shot us off to the MO where I was inoculated and vaccinated and labelled yet again as fit for overseas service. My brain retreated into panic thinking of the thousands of things I had to plan and do.

Back at Phyllis Court I was faced with the luggage question. I wasn't able to discover how much I could take, but everyone said not much. So I sat on the floor in my bedroom with my worldly goods in a high circle around me and packed all my stuff into suitcases, tidied myself up and tottered down exhausted to dinner and found my stomach too sick inside to be able to eat.

After dinner our taxi came and Robbie and I and our many cases began a hellish journey through the rain and blackout up to town and I went to the Goldies. There I sat round the fire eating ham sandwiches and learning about how Bunty is now engaged to Stanley and swapping with her a lot of my unwanted woollies for talcum powder and face flannels. We went to bed at two, I didn't sleep for hours after, then had to get up at seven to catch the 9.05 train up to Cheltenham. I was still too busy to be able to think about what was happening to me.

Today up here I have been buying the rest of the things I'll need, like lots of soap and toothpaste and dungarees for deck and glucose for when I'm sick and a lock for my kitbag and a new suitcase and a key ring, also I've sent off lots of telegrams: to my friends and to my tailor about tropical kit.

This morning we heard the news that Japan had declared war on us and the Americans. Well, everyone's in it now. I'm glad the Americans are, we hadn't been liking them too well lately and that's been a bad thing.

171

Together we are the hope of the world and the war will unite us in the way it unites all strangers fighting for the same cause, and after we shall truly be brothers. If they had never fought as we had, no matter how much they helped us in other ways, the barrier would still be between us, and our dislike would have grown. I shall always in the future try to remember that though their cockiness and conceit does sometimes jar, at least they are unafraid to say 'go to hell' to those against us and they will never compromise or crawl in their dealings with their enemies. We shall be one and in us lies the hope of the world.

20 December 1941

I spent a farewell evening last night with the Cunninghams and got back here after lunch today, to find with incredulous delighted joy that our signal was through and we leave here for our depot and the first stage of our journey on the 29th. I can't really believe it, to be travelling at last and going so far and to such strange places. I want to shout and yell and dance till I drop but I mustn't be too juvenile.

22 December 1941

Today our instructions came for us from the Air Ministry in the shape of sheets of typescript telling us of the lamentable qualities of Eastern servants and of the hordes of 'wellie beans' and silver fish, bedbugs and other hordes of horrors which apparently abound in Egypt and are waiting, ready to eat their swift way through all our possessions and presumably our persons. So in horror I fled to buy Keetings and mothballs, to put up some sort of defensive action against their onslaught. And I am the type of person who'd sooner sleep on the floor than share her bed with a spider, and who flees from an earwig. Out there also, according to the Air Ministry, our shoes are an alluring nest for scorpions. The girls who sneered at my previous purchase of tropical kit have now spent exhausting days battling through Christmas crowds to get uniforms, which have practically all gone to the ATS anyway, while I sit back, smug and self-satisfied and go out and buy another bottle of anti-insect lotion. I also try on now and again my topee,[19] give a brief unhappy look at the result and put it away to wait for more courage to try again. However many surplus men there may be in the desert and on the troopship I don't think I, in my topee, tropical kit (khaki is not my colour), smothered in mosquito bites and fifty million freckles and smelling vilely of my anti-everything ointment, am going to be much of a hit with anyone.

2 January 1942

On Monday our signal came through saying we were to report to Liverpool before four o'clock on the 9th. So

---

[19] A pith helmet worn by troops in the Tropics.

that evening I had a frenzy of packing and prepared to go up and see Mother again, my really final five days' leave. And on the Tuesday morning Mary[20] and I drove precariously to Maidenhead in the car she had just bought from Helby[21] for £15 on which she couldn't work out how to reverse and this was the first time she had driven it any distance at all. And from there we caught a train to town.

We ate a heavenly and delicious and utterly satisfying lunch at Leon's, the Chinese restaurant, and went in the afternoon to see *Dumbo*, the new Walt Disney, not as good as *Pinocchio* or *Snow White*.

We stayed overnight at a hotel near Paddington and the next morning she returned to Medmenham and I came up to Cheltenham, where I seemed to spend all the time doing last bits of shopping and I began to have nightmares in earnest about packing and the financial state.

6 January 1942

At the nasty hour of 6.30 this morning, I tottered from bed and dressed and packed, on my last morning at Phyllis Court.

We got to the station at 7.48 and the train left at 7.50! Somehow I persuaded a grumbling, protesting porter to hurl our trunks and cases and kitbags into the luggage van, while Helby ran like a hare to a carriage bearing all

---

[20] Mary Bowden.
[21] Rosemary Helby who also accompanied me to Egypt.

174

our oddments. The train left even as our feet reached inside it and we were left with the most embarrassing array of oddments to be exposed to a surprised world of Paddington. So that at Twyford, Helby had to leap from the compartment to the luggage van to pack them in her spare kitbag before a grinning guard.

The journey from Euston to Liverpool was comparatively uneventful, except that a coffin on the train (full!) prevented us from getting through to the dining car so that our sandwiches had to be inadequately doled out to six starving WAAF officers.

At Lime Street chaos came. After much time and much more trouble we found our respective luggage, and also a man with a lorry who vanished into Liverpool with it all. Everyone else organised themselves taxis. We, after snapping our fingers in vain for a very long time, went to the embarkation offices by tram. There we were told to go to the Adelphi Hotel and be ready with our luggage labelled to leave at nine o'clock the next morning.

Then I had dinner and am sitting writing this in the residents lounge. I still cannot believe that tomorrow it happens to me, my dearest and strongest dream: I begin at twenty-two to travel and in future when others talk casually of distant places, I need never rail against circumstances which kept me always in England.

Events of 1941

14 February The first units of the German Afrika Korps, under Erwin Rommel, landed in North Africa.

10 May 1500 were killed and 1800 wounded on the final, and heaviest, night of bombing over London.

27 May German battleship *Bismarck* was sunk by British warships with the loss of 2000 men.

1 June Britain began to ration clothes. Civilians were issued with sufficient coupons to purchase one entire outfit every year, and were requested to 'make do and mend'.

22 June Germany invaded Russia, employing three million troops over a thousand-mile front.

3 September Nazis tested gas chambers for the first time, killing 600 Soviet prisoners of war at Auschwitz.

29 September Nazis began the massacre of Jews in Kiev.

7 December US base at Pearl Harbor was attacked by Japanese bombers, leaving 2400 American sailors dead or missing.

8 December USA and Britain declared war on Japan.

11 December Germany and Italy declared war on USA.

18 December Britain conscripted all unmarried women aged between twenty and thirty.

PART III

Egypt

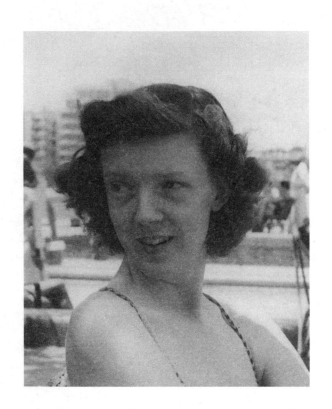

1942

7 January 1942

Well, here we are on board. The ship is the SS *Otranto*, Orient Line. We were to be ready for collection, they told us, at nine o'clock. By 10.30 we were still waiting and there was a thick fog outside, giving birth to the thought that we might be left for another night at the Adelphi. However, by 11.30 we were all in our bus, our luggage having vanished into the fog in front of us. Our luggage has been the cause of indescribable toil and trouble to us.

By twelve o'clock we were walking up the gangway and swiftly after were in our cabins. Ours is an L-shaped room with five bunks in it. By a colossal piece of luck I am in a bunk by itself and the one with a porthole, so that I have the windowsill extra to rest things on and a bedside cupboard none of the others possesses. So I am going to be comparatively comfortable.

After a large and luscious lunch, indicating that rationing has left the ship untouched, Elizabeth,[1] Diana[2] and I

[1] Elizabeth Hemelrick.
[2] Diana Ovlebar.

went out on the deck and leant over the side to watch the troops coming aboard and the men putting our luggage on board, by means of an insecure-looking rope-hammock affair. We were also interested to note that carpenters are still erecting large numbers of bunks, so it doesn't seem that we'll be sailing for a day or so and now we are prisoners on board and under no circumstances may go ashore again.

Then there was tea and the unpacking of our luggage. And then an even larger dinner, complete with oranges, so that unless we are very strong-minded we shall ultimately land in Cairo bloated pigs.

Now we are sitting in the lounge where I write this, waiting for one of the officers to talk to us on things we should know. I am surprised and a little shocked at my absence of emotion over all that has happened. Before the war I would have gone mad with excitement and joy if circumstances had gratified the greatest of my aspirations and set me on a Channel steamer; now here I am en route for Africa and I feel no excitement at all. As I am now, I feel the rich, full present is rushing across my life and I am not enjoying it or tasting it to half its capacities and I do so detest blasé people.

Oh yes, the thing I forgot to say is that cigarettes on board are eightpence for twenty and pink gins twopence halfpenny and whisky fourpence, so that I shall probably take to smoking again and look like cultivating drink in a big way.

8 January 1942

Our second day on board and still we stay in port. However, we seem to be considerably nearer sailing. We have been ordered tonight to sleep in our clothes, a process we have to go on doing for some weeks apparently and as a result here we all are, in slacks and jumpers etc., with rugs and water bottles and such of our possessions as we love most dearly beside our beds, just like the days of the Blitz again. I do so detest sleeping in my clothes, but I see their point most clearly and obey without protest. The strongest rumour pins our sailing date to tonight or tomorrow night. The hopeful party say tonight, but reason and sober observation and judgement make tomorrow a better favourite. Still we can't help hoping it is tonight and we keep thinking we hear 'on our way' noises.

We spent the morning watching stores being loaded on and in the afternoon more troops streamed aboard. And they removed the letterbox containing going ashore letters which is the strongest point in favour of departure tonight. Already the RAF and Army are mingling with the WAAF. Diana, Elizabeth and myself passed the evening with some members of a coastal command squadron, but by their looks at least, all the men aboard seemed a pretty ropy crowd or else perhaps I'm getting more selective. The ones we met were the average hard-drinking, line-shooting[3] pilots, with less than usual charm; the charm

---

[3] To shoot a line is to tell a story boastfully.

which in the past has blinded me to all their faults. Only perhaps it is because of me being altered and not them that they have no charm any more. So I just shot a slick, meaningless line and inside was lonely and outside gay and refused an offer of a walk on deck and came to bed early, which I was pleased with myself about and now I must sleep. I meant to write lots describing the docks and the dockers and the ship in more detail but I've plenty of time in the days to come.

10 January 1942

I should have written about yesterday last night but I was too tired to do so. All the morning we had boat drill, which proved very exhausting, especially the wearing of life jackets. Just after lunch we started to sail, it consisted only of leaving the dock to anchor in the river but it was wildly exciting. We put on all our reserves of warm clothing and went out on the deck where the sights were thrilling but the wind bitterly cold. Looking at the sea for a brief moment I had that feeling of insecure suspension on the edge of destruction like I get at the start of a flight when there is only a thin structure between myself and space. However, it soon passed and the ship is so large (to me anyway, it is 23,000 tonnes) that most of the time (so far) I forget it's a ship at all.

The river is far more exciting than the docks. There were other ships to see: our sister ship the *Orontes*, tugs and trawlers and even a corvette. Only when we were frozen beyond endurance did we go inside to pass an hilarious evening in the lounge with our two pilot acquaintances, who shed to some degree their previous bad-type lines, played Draw the Well Dry[4] with us and gave us elementary lessons in astro-navigation. Then in return for our washing of socks and collars they are organising their batmen[5] into cleaning our buttons and shoes.

12 January 1942

I shall probably be removed in the middle of this to go to the beastly boat drill but I can start it at least. We are now properly on our way and at the present moment are sailing round the north of Ireland. Yesterday the sea was incredibly calm but today it is much rougher and already one WAAF has felt queasy and has borrowed a spoonful of my glucose. Diana and I went up upon deck directly after breakfast and watched the sky stop being night and the dark cruel water rolling around us. So far I don't feel sick at all, but I am not conceited enough to be sure that I won't later be. The days have so far been spent walking on the deck in the daylight and in social intercourse in the evening. People are beginning to know each other. Diana and I already know the majority of 221 Squadron. The nicest and most interesting of them are the two Peters, aged twenty-seven and thirty respectively, and both large flying officer air gunners. I met them before lunch yesterday in the lounge when they bought me orangeade. In the

[4] A card game also known as Beggar My Neighbour.
[5] Batmen were the servants assigned to all male officers.

evening they bought me peach and cherry brandies and talked most interestingly about books and people. I like both of them very much but because they are both older and more intelligent than myself I do not wish to foist myself unwanted on them but must proceed slowly with what I hope will become a friendship. Then there is the squadron's Irish doctor whom we like very much and a number of lesser-known pilots of relatively attractive appearances.

Since I started writing this the sea has got much rougher. Quite a number of people are ill now and we have just returned from a totter up to the boat deck, battling against wind and rain and spray and seeing the horizon and the rest of the convoy rise and vanish in the most spectacular manner. According to the crew, this present tempest is only a slight swell but a real storm will arise by tonight. I am not sick or feeling like it yet, but I am not boasting.

13 January 1942

Well, it went on getting even rougher and still continues to be simply beastly with, according to the Fourth Officer, little hope of any alteration for at least two more days. Our numbers at meals have thinned beyond belief. I felt fine until about ten minutes before dinner, when I had a very uneasy few moments of battling against nausea with will-power, the former of which gets stronger hourly and the latter alas weaker, despite its fortification with glucose and brandy and ginger wine.

That time will-power won and I walked down to dinner with the nicer of the two Peters, basking in his admiration and his advice as to what I should eat. I managed to eat fish and then potatoes and greens and a couple of rolls and watched, with an admiration flecked with hatred, a girl at the next table eating all her dinner, including (with relish) asparagus. However, I took comfort at the sight of so many empty chairs; at least I was there.

After dinner I did feel much better and was able to spend a short but pleasant evening chatting to the very nice Peter about what both of us did pre-war, then taking a turn on deck after to look at the phosphorescence.

In the night it got rougher. We were woken soon after two by practically everything we possessed falling down and breaking and by the screams of Jane who received Helby's heavy book on her head, being unfortunate enough to sleep under Helby and the collection of weighty knick-knacks Helby finds necessary to surround herself with before sleep. Still we consoled her by saying that it might have been Helby's torch, a large instrument, or even Helby – a very solid individual – and we laughed merrily and unkindly at the thought of Helby bouncing from off Jane's head.

Now this morning it is even rougher. I made breakfast but only ate toast and marmalade and toyed with a little tea, as I haven't been on deck and am now reclining on my bunk. I shall be surprised today if I'm not sick.

15 January 1942

All of a sudden I got my sea legs after never having once been sick and saved only from outrageous conceit by the knowledge that twice I did feel simply lousy. Most people are better by now and emerged from the sick seclusion of their cabins and the days have settled into a regular routine of breakfast and boat drill and a walk on deck and lunch and another walk after and a read and a sleep until dinner and a little social chatter in the lounge before an early bed. We shall enjoy it better when it gets hot and we can sunbathe all day on deck, though now it is amazing how quickly the hours pass, just watching the water and the rest of the convoy and letting your hair get ripped by the wind. I am feeling tremendously fit now and enjoying very much the company of 221 Squadron, especially of the two Peters, both of whom I take the best views of.

Last night the even tenor of our days was shaken a little by the ship's steering device breaking and causing us to be unable to keep up with the rest of the convoy. This happened at about eleven in the evening and we knew nothing of it except to have our sleep momentarily disturbed by a lot of creaking and wailing and odd sorts of sounds.

In the morning, however, Robbie went on deck and came back to tell us, her incredulous listeners, that the convoy had gone. At breakfast our steward told us the whole story and expressed hopes, unshared by us, that we should have to return to England, causing us to wonder

186

whether perhaps we wouldn't put in to New York for repairs, being this morning nearer the American side of the Atlantic (wishful thinking).

But they mended the thing and by lunchtime we were in the convoy again and now I must have my salt-water bath and get ready for yet another enormous and unnecessary meal.

16 January 1942

Yesterday evening was wonderful. As I was going up into the lounge from my cabin Peter came up behind me taking hold of the strings of my life jacket and walking over with me to get our coffee. And we sat the whole evening together on one of the couches while he showed me on an atlas the places in the world he had been to and told me about a trip he had done as an air gunner taking Harry Hopkins[6] to Russia and spending a week in Archangel and all the food the Russians had given them to eat.

The sea was still rough and the ship pitched around a lot. Two people were thrown over from their chairs. I do so like Peter, he's tall and very dark with bright blue eyes and an enchanting smile and is more a Noël Cowardy sort of person than a very out-in-the-open-airy one. I have to take myself firmly in hand with reminders about the unlastingness of ship friendships and general undesirability

---

[6] Harry Hopkins (1890–1946): American politician and one of President Roosevelt's closest advisers.

of love, because I don't want to be in anguish for ages after he's gone again. However, time will show and take its course and I don't suppose it will kill me.

Today there was quite some excitement. I was walking with a nice little radio operator on the boat deck when the alert signal was given and we had to take cover against a Condor seen flying near the convoy. Waiting in my cabin we heard our ship's guns but it was some hours before the aircraft finally flew off and we are wondering now just how many submarines it has reported our positions to, time again will show that too. I am fairly used to being bombed but to be torpedoed is an unknown, and therefore nastier, horror.

17 January 1942

Life is really most exhilarating. I have rarely felt more alive and happy and gay.

Last night I had another most interesting conversation with my very nice Peter, this time about books and plays and the ballet and the London theatre, so that the two years of war were gone and all my old desires and ambitions stirred inside me again. He is such an interesting and intelligent person and he doesn't patronise which he might well do, being thirty and knowing so much more about everything than I do. And when we went to bed that evening we dressed more thoroughly than usual and prepared with more care our shipwreck bags in case the Condor had reported our positions to lurking enemy submarines. But the night was uneventful and in the morning we found the battleship *Resolution* had joined the convoy and was only about two cables away from our starboard side. We were enchanted with it and leant over the rail to study it thoroughly, noting the camouflage, its aircraft and its guns.

We passed the afternoon in exhilarating argument on deck with the other Peter, whom I better call Max for clarity's sake like the rest of his squadron do, on the importance of aerial photography in relation to intelligence gleaned from other sources. We came out of the argument rather badly but Max is a very good arguer and makes you mad with patronage and insult so that you get heated and incoherent.

Our position is now somewhere round the Azores and the weather is getting warmer. I have shed practically all my woollies and the day when I can appear in my glamorous blue sunglasses and my dashing boiler suit and Aertex shirt becomes a possibility. We should also be in Freetown in about a week unless that Condor makes us alter our course very considerably.

20 January 1942

The weather is really hot now and I think we'll be in our tropical kit in a day or so. WAAFs have been devoting hours to the cutting down, reshaping and resewing of the men's tropical kit, most of which was issued to them from stores and the Air Ministry's ideas on tailoring are the least bit elementary. Even I have entirely reorganised and perfected two shirts for my nice Peter and put his air gunner's badge on his tunic for him.

Today we were nearly all the time on deck, in the afternoon wearing slacks and Aertex shirts and sunning ourselves most enjoyably. And in the evening I played deck tennis with Peter and Max and the ship's medical officer with the result that I am now writing this sleepily in bed at the early hour of a quarter to ten – only it is really quarter to eleven as we are now sailing east again so the clocks go on an hour. Otherwise, there is nothing untoward or exciting to report except that last night Peter and I watched the most beautiful sunset I have ever seen: the sun actually seemed to go down into the sea, which was silver and molten and unrippled, and the ships silhouetted black on it like motionless toys. And I cannot begin to describe the surrounding sky or the colours that stained it.

It was beautiful again tonight when Peter and I went out to see the crescent moon and the thousand stars and the white on the water where the ship cut her way and down at the stern the troops were on deck shadowing the darkness, singing sea shanties accompanied by an accordion.

We heard too yesterday a little more exciting news about that Condor which visited us. Apparently before it came to us it had tried to bomb the convoy straggler separated from us by earlier bad weather and had damaged its steering gear with a near miss so that the ship with its 2000 odd troops on board had had to put in for repairs at the Azores which we passed a few days ago. And apparently if they stayed there more than thirty-six hours they were all capable of being interned so that with its destroyer escort it was contemplating a dash for Gibraltar.

Finally, we should be in Freetown by about Saturday.

23 January 1942

We went into tropical kit yesterday. It is not a particularly becoming uniform but it is both comfortable and cool. Only, of course, in the two days during which we have worn it the sun has been cloud-coated and a howling wind has raged. It gets hotter at nights and last night I woke up in a black, small and stifling cabin to the sensations almost of a nightmare.

We were issued today with tins of anti-mosquito ointment and as we are due to arrive at Freetown tomorrow some time and will probably anchor outside for a few days we shall be glad of what protection it can give us. Unfortunately we shan't be allowed to land at Freetown as there is a danger of contracting yellow fever so a pretty boring and tantalising few days are before us while we put in there. This is supposed to be the most dangerous part of our journey and the cheerful story which is circulating is that at least two ships in every convoy are sunk outside Freetown. However, the only excitement to date has been the sounding of a 'take cover' at the appearance of a Sunderland flying boat, presumably part of the convoy patrol now looking after us. It's a good thing we've got something with us now as our battleship left us the other night, no doubt, as one of our RAF chums remarked bitterly, 'because its position, snug in the middle of the convoy and protected by us from any torpedoes was no longer safe enough for it'.

All the officers on board are spending nearly all their time censoring the men's letters which can be posted from Freetown. Otherwise, little untoward happens, our days are the same round of sleeping and eating and drinking and social chatter.

There was a party last night in the lounge where everybody worked off their respective oppression caused by the ship's confining quarters by singing lustily at the two pianos, but it wasn't madly amusing. After Freetown we are promised dancing and films and they will be welcome.

26 January 1942

Yesterday just before lunch we arrived at Freetown. We all went out onto the decks to watch and there for the first time I saw and still cannot believe it, Africa. It's been too easy to get to it, it's been too little a while since I was always all my life in England.

We anchored well up the river with the rest of the convoy and the coast is only a slight stretch of water away. There are hills covered with scrub and the immediate shore is fringed sparsely with trees, among which we delightedly picked out our first palm tree. There are a few buildings and seaplanes are moored in the river. That is about all we can see of the place and as none of us is to be given any shore leave here because of its disease-ridden climate we aren't likely to see any more of it. Rumour reports that we anchor here for four days or until next Thursday. Whereas it is good to see land again, to be able to abandon the perpetual carrying of our life jackets and to have to endure only a partial blackout, it is not so enjoyable to be forbidden to take a bath because of the undesirable conditions of the river and the heat at night is exhausting; we have no energy at all for anything.

In the day, I must admit, it is not too intolerable and we passed a most entertaining day yesterday, leaning over the rail watching the efforts of the native bum boats selling bananas (the first we've seen for months), coconuts, mangoes and miserable still-alive chickens to troops strictly forbidden to buy anything from them. I must say I wasn't tempted. The natives were a scrofulous-looking crew with obviously a total absence of any sort of personal hygiene, though looking picturesque enough in the colourful rags they wore, paddling their flimsy boats with gaily painted paddles and some of them dived into the water after sixpences, showing enough business instinct to refuse to dive for pennies. And at night we watched the sun sink in a matter of minutes beyond the hills, round and red, its last reflections glinting in the green water. I don't think, though, that I am going to like the heat.

27 January 1942

Two nights ago they gave a dance up on the boat deck under the awning, illuminated by the partial blackout allowed us while in harbour until half past ten. It was a great success and colossal fun. The OC[7] troops gave us permission to wear civilian clothes and Diana and I danced every dance to a state of exhaustion. There was lots of room on the deck and in the intervals you could move from the awning onto the dark of the unlighted deck and lean over the rails to watch the water and the bonfires and the lights of Freetown and our sister ships. And after we went back into the lounge, drank iced lemonade and then sang for about an hour round the piano, while standing beside our dear dear Peter Thirtle who sings well enough to keep even me in tune.

The next night one of the officers took Diana and me up on the boat deck to see the film which was being shown to the men. It was a ghastly film, an incredibly old Joe E. Brown and I thought an insult, the sort of insult entertainment people always seem to make, basing their ideas on brutal and licentious soldiery as compared with the intelligence of a lot of normal individuals. But it was interesting to see a film in the open air and better than sitting in a suffocating lounge. Then, when we came down we were invited to a party given by the bunch of Sunderland Squadron boys who had come aboard but we were too tired to enjoy ourselves greatly and are sleeping this afternoon in anticipation of another dance tonight which can only happen if we don't sail. As there are rumours of fresh passengers coming aboard and none has

[7] Officer Commanding.

so far arrived, I don't think our departure today is likely somehow.

The rest of the days we sunbathe on deck and drink endless delicious fruit drinks. The Tropics are fine so long as you don't have to work. I don't even have to wash my own stockings any more.[8]

30 January 1942

The night before we left Freetown some of the pilots from the shore station came on board and we gave a party for them. After, when their launch had come to collect them, they asked us to go for a trip in it round the harbour. The group captain and the wing commander were luckily with us and allowed themselves to be persuaded into it and came along too.

We crowded into the launch and stood there, our hair blowing as the white foam sprang up either side of the cut we made in the sea. We went over to another ship called, I think, *Christian Holstein*, collected another party from there and then returned reluctantly to the *Otranto*. There would have been a colossal row about the escapade as the ship's officer unfortunately heard about it. But the presence of the Group Captain fortunately neutralized it to nothing. The next day we left Freetown, passing the

[8] The Other Ranks on board lived in appalling conditions. Those few with pre-war domestic skills such as hairdressing, laundry etc. escaped briefly to work for the female officers who did not have batmen.

afternoon watching the disappearing coast of West Africa until we were through the boom and out into the sea.

Today some time we are due to cross the line. It is hot but not quite so hot as I had imagined the Equator to be and the days still passed delightfully and lazily in the company of pleasant people. There are our perfect Peters, especially Peter Thirtle, and Robert and Alec whom I met at the dance, with whom we passed the days so contentedly.

1 February 1942

Yesterday afternoon at 3.40 we crossed the Equator. I was asleep on the deck with Alec and Diana and Robert when I was woken at the crucial moment to look at the sea and to think – this is the Equator. In life's usual anticlimactic way it was the coldest day since we'd come to the Tropics and Diana and I were actually glad of a rug round our legs. However, I had now crossed the line, even if (because this is a troopship in the war) there were none of the usual crossing-the-line ceremonies. And in the evening there was a dance by moonlight on the boat deck to gramophone records. The moon was high and white and full and beautiful and there was a welcome wind blowing, just a little too vigorously, through the skirt of my frock. Alec and I sat out one dance and went up to the prow of the ship, standing there to let the wind push back my hair and billow my dress. The ship in the moonlight, white foam on the water, is the most romantic and beautiful sight, like all the book descriptions which you might have thought exaggerated, but which still do not capture the reality. The men were sleeping all over the lower decks. It's a good thing that they can now do so. Their quarters on board, I am told, are disgraceful, being overcrowded, under-ventilated and squalid.[9]

4 February 1942

I will describe a day, taking yesterday as a both typical and pleasant example.

In the morning after we are woken by our steward, there is the usual cramming of five baths into the hour between seven, when we wake, and eight, which is breakfast. As I hate getting up early I am invariably last to the bath and equally inevitably late for breakfast which these days is enriched by such exotic, un-English dishes as pawpaw. And after breakfast I go out onto the deck where on the day under description I stood between Max and Alec, watching the flying fish which came out in shoals from the water as the ship approached them.

Then at 10.30 there is the brief unpleasantness of boat drill, after which Diana and I go and sit with our books in the lounge, joined in due course by our friends who buy

---

[9] One of Churchill's secretaries, John Colville, was on board below deck with rank and file soldiers. The conditions were so bad that he wrote to Churchill's wife warning of a mutiny. As a result, Churchill ensured better below-deck conditions thenceforth. See Colville's diaries, *The Fringes of Power* (Weidenfield & Nicolson, 2004).

drinks and chatter entertainingly until it is one o'clock and lunchtime. The morning is perfect if Peter Thirtle joins the circle so yesterday's one black spot was because he did not. And after lunch I went on deck with sundry rugs and books and sweets and oranges and topees and sunglasses and made myself comfortable with Alec and Diana to sleep until nearly four. Then Alec had to go away to give a lecture to his men and Diana was having a German lesson a little way up the deck with Robert and to my satisfaction Peter Thirtle came over and talked to me. The conversation, though, was somewhat depressing. He thinks things will be the same, only worse and more so, in England after the war. The people controlling money and industry will continue to keep their hold on their power; there will be even sharper class distinction; and all the reforms I hoped would happen will never come. He says he won't have anything to do with politics after the war but become a barrister. I think it's a dreadful and depressing thing if the men with ideals and intelligence are already so disillusioned that they will not even fight for the future. And then Diana came over and Roger, another Army officer, and we played a game of Deck-Quoits,[10] going down to the lounge after for a drink before dinner.

After dinner there was a dance and, tired, at 11.30 I went to bed.

[10] A game in which rope rings are thrown onto a marked-out board on deck.

7 February 1942

The night before last the sergeants on board gave a dance and invited the WAAFs and nurses to it. After dinner we were played from the lounge to the tune of 'Goodnight Ladies' by the officers who then settled themselves down to a truly colossal stag party, the noise of which penetrated even to our party, which was progressing slightly more decorously in B deck square. It followed, from what I was later told, the usual pattern: singing low songs, leaping round the room over furniture, fighting unbitterly and drinking heavily. It worked off whatever suppressed energies they may have had. The next day there were a lot of very subdued-looking men and most of them had the grace to admit that it was a very good thing for them financially and in every other way that the restraining presence of the ladies was there every other night.

We in the Sergeants Mess were also having fun. The sergeants could certainly dance and I for one enjoyed the break from always the same faces.

At about eleven (the OC troops had to keep on giving extensions to us) the dance ended and one of the sergeants gave his party rendering of Hitler, for which he made up his face most realistically and was very very funny. I was standing at the back of the room with Jock and three of his sergeants when someone said, 'Hello, Joan.' And there behind me was Max with his black hair curling and his blue eyes even bluer, with Peter Thirtle and Alec. I stood on a chair with the three of them around me and laughed at the sergeant giving a Hitler speech to which we cheered and booed and *sieg heiled* and *heil Hitlered* and sang 'Deutschland Über Alles' with every gusto. Then unfortunately the unpleasant adjutant in a Jaeger dressing gown and a very sour expression, entered, and quite soon after that the party broke up.

12 February 1942

The four days in Durban I shall never forget. For four days we were in a town untouched with war, a perfect and beautiful town. The first day Alec, Diana, Harry and I walked through its streets, sightseeing, and had dinner in the evening at the Edward Hotel which looks over the promenade to the sea. And in the Edward we met Peter Thirtle for a drink where he gave me a present of two chiffon scarves.

The second day I went with Peter and Max to the bank in the morning, with Elizabeth, Diana, Roger and the doctor to bathe in the afternoon and have tea at the Edward, and in the evening went back to the ship, as Alec was orderly officer.

Alec and I went up to the deserted boat deck watching the lights of the town and realising both of us we could be falling in love.

Sunday was perhaps the most perfect. We went out in a coach, Alec and I, Elizabeth, Roger, Diana and Max, out to the Thousand Hills, the scenery of which was in no way comparable with the best of England but which was interesting and novel to see, particularly when we were taken round a Zulu settlement.

We had lunch at a hotel on the way and after it Alec and I walked up a white steep sunshine-brightened road, on the banks of which were growing strange bushes, under whose shade natives were sprawled in coloured clothes and among the grass were large, fantastically coloured grasshoppers.

The evening was the most perfect. Alec and I had dinner together at the Edward and then took a rickshaw up the promenade for a long way past the houses and the light to just green bushes and the sea.

Then we got out of the rickshaw and walked back. We sat down together on the white soft sand by the sea and a long while after we walked back to the hotel, holding hands with contentment so deep inside us even the knowledge that so soon we must leave here could not touch our peace. I pretended that we were walking back to our home, that we lived here always, in one of those flats in that block so brilliantly lit and that every night of our lives we could go out and see the lights and never be in any war. Only I was too happy to regret deeply that none of these things were mine.

The last day I met Alec at the Edward Hotel, put on my new green frock for him and he gave me roses and carnations and lily of the valley scent. And then went with him, Roger and Diana to a heavenly hotel on a hill, called the Caister, for dinner. Finished the evening off at the fair and then when Roger and Diana had gone paddled on the beach until it was time to return.

The next morning we sailed and the ship now is crammed to discomfort with so many new arrivals and also now, each day, I see coming the day when Alec will have to leave me. He is twenty-seven in March, tall and thinnish and not very dark and the shape of his face is a little like mine because several people have remarked that we look like brother and sister.

25 February 1942

I am writing this from my bunk where about the first of the climate diseases has laid me low along with a good 25 per cent of the rest of the ship's company. I will not dwell on the more sordid side effects of the affliction but will just mention that at the climax of its awfulness, which was eleven o'clock the day before yesterday evening, I lay moaning on my bunk, a thousand rasping spears thrusting through my stomach, a roaring in my ears, a blackness in my head, pins and needles in my arms and legs and a flaming heat consuming all. The agony has now gone and I am left limp and exhausted and forgetting the taste of food and hoping that soon I'll be allowed to get up again.

28 February 1942

Yesterday afternoon there was a boxing tournament which we watched from the far end of A deck, I in a deckchair and Alec lying on his stomach on both our rugs. The lower decks were crowded with men and there were men up the riggings, on the ship's rails and even on the awnings. We watched from two till six and then went down to prepare for an early dinner as there was a dance on the boat deck at 7.30.

At the dance Alec said to me, 'We'll be at Aden tomorrow and it's Suez by about Thursday.' Because I cannot bear to think about a life again where he is not with me all the time I refuse to let myself realise what he said, that it is only days now before we arrive.

After the dance we went back to the lounge and sat with Jock trying in vain to get drinks from the steward which, since these new arrivals, takes at least two hours.

I have wondered sometimes whether I am not just someone Alec's fond of, perhaps he loves in an unemotional well-under-control way, in that all his passion went to his first love, a girl he was engaged to when he was twenty-one and who at the last minute let him down and refused to marry him.

3 March 1942

We put in to Aden two days ago, arriving in the afternoon and leaving again some time the next night. A few people got ashore. I wasn't one of them but then I don't toady. It didn't look a particularly prepossessing place, only rocks and a few dusty bits of greenery. But I would have liked to have said that I had been ashore, rather like the time when I crawled round the fiery furnace of the *Otranto*'s engine rooms; the satisfaction then being the telling of it afterwards.

Alec and I sat on the boat deck after dinner and watched the town lights and talked together contentedly and now we are fairly rushing up the Red Sea to arrive, so rumour has it, at Suez on Thursday. The end of these weeks of our journey, already the nightmare of packing and luggage coping has begun again and our money has been taken away to be converted into Egyptian currency.

11 March 1942

After lunch a launch brought an accountant officer on board and at five o'clock the WAAFs and the nurses were in the ferry going across the sea to Suez.

Suez had been bombed for the last few nights they told us, so we were being taken off the ship at unbelievable and breakneck speed.

The journey from Suez to Cairo was long and cold in a dirty, comfortless train. And we arrived at 11.30 at night, to be met by a Squadron Flight and Assistant Section Officer and taken to the Continental Hotel where, after sandwiches and coffee, we eventually got to bed at after one.

The next day we were awoken by Squadron Leader Glyn Daniel[11] walking into our bedroom, when the last we had seen of him (and where we still imagined him to be) was at Medmenham. He was flying to India and had one more day in Cairo, so he took us to Groppi's[12] for coffee and to Marconi's and the bank. And in the

[11] Glyn Daniel (1914–86): a well-known archaeologist.
[12] Groppi's is still a well-known coffee shop in Cairo.

afternoon we went out to Heliopolis to see the PRU[13] crowd and in the evening Leo Hands, Denis Belleby and Philip Date, all of whom we knew and worked with in England, came over and took us to dinner where there was dancing and a very bad cabaret.

Next day Alec called at the hotel (which we hated) and he and I went shopping around Cairo and to a cinema which had additional dialogue in French and Arabic and Greek. Alec is at the BDRA[14] until he is sent out to the desert and it is near Heliopolis aerodrome where we now work. And on Sunday we went to the races where we both lost money, only he more than me because really the gambling spirit is not in my blood.

On Monday we started to work, which we do from eight till one and four till seven, only at the moment they are in chaos about us and there is nothing much for us to do. I was first in the Italy section and am now in Turkey with Denis Belleby, whom I like very much.[15] We're living now at the Heliopolis Hotel, which is only a very little better than the Continental, and our luggage has at last arrived.

I have met Sue Perry out here, with whom I joined the WAAFs so long ago in those early war days in Hendon.

---

[13] Photographic Reconnaissance Unit.
[14] A centre from which men were posted.
[15] Ultimately, our task in Egypt would be to interpret aerial photographs taken by the unit's Beaufighter pilots over the western desert and the Mediterranean, exactly the same work as in the UK except that the terrain revealed in the photographs was very different from the European landscape.

And today Diana looked up some friends of Glyn's who live in Heliopolis.

21 March 1942

I languish in bed with sandfly fever, my temperature obstinately rising a degree each night so that the next morning, despite the fact that the beastly thing is by this time quite normal, the doctors won't let me get up. It looks like this kind of thing can go on quite indefinitely.

Today after lunch I woke to have the Sister tell me two visitors had come and without much interest I combed out my hair and powdered my nose. In walked Diana and Captain Mortimer Lloyd. Captain Lloyd we met on the aerodrome where he spends part of his time and he is tall, handsome and very dashing. Much is my silent horror that he should be seeing me now looking so foul but I felt considerably elated that he had come and had brought me chocolates and creamy cakes. Then he had to go, with promises of a return visit, and Diana stayed on, eating my chocolates and gossiping of this and that.

A little while after Sister came in and said, 'Another visitor for you: the only one who has ever come at the right time,' with an angry glare. I am not a very popular patient; I don't stay under my towel enough inhaling, and my visitors do everything wrong: they put cigarette ash in the flower vases and make much too much noise. And in walked Alec. I cannot describe my surprise. His major was coming into Cairo on leave and had given him a lift in and the car was taking him back at eleven. I'll leave you to imagine my fury and anguish and torment at being incarcerated here in bed and even as I write these lines he and his major will be in the Heliopolis House Hotel having dinner with Diana and Elizabeth. Life sometimes is a bitter thing. He has apparently struck a very good thing at Suez and likes life there a lot, only he seems to think they'll be moving to the front quite soon. He looked very fit and quite smug and exuded self-satisfaction. I vowed to take him down considerably more than just one peg. Captain Lloyd will be the very thing with which to shake him – oh, and he ate the other half of my chocolates!

25 March 1942

Bored, bad-tempered and browned off, I am still a prisoner in my hospital bed. Every night my unmentionable temperature rises and every morning it is back to normal again. The hospital staff are now getting thoroughly interested in the phenomenon. The colonel today examined me minutely from top to toe, questioning me in embarrassing detail about my personal habits, but could find nothing wrong with the works. The female doctor took swabs, painfully, of both my nostrils. The throat and nose specialist paid me two visits, on the first of which he peered up my wretched nose with lights and forceps, and in the second he told me he was going to have it X-rayed. In the interludes I sniff up saline sniffs (an embarrassing and revolting procedure), inhale, eat heartily and feel comparatively fine. Still at night my temperature rises, as I've said before there's no apparent end to this sort of thing.

I read a lot, I write a few letters, I chat to my co-sufferers, made more interesting by the arrival of a VAD[16] who can speak Arabic, a nursing sister with a gramophone and an ancient selection of Hutch[17] records, and a WAAF who escaped from Yugoslavia and Greece some twenty-four hours in front of the Germans.

Between 3.30 and 5.30 we have our visitors. Yesterday Elizabeth and Diana rushed into the room announcing that they had taken a flat with three bedrooms and lots of green furniture, with no hot water, very near the aerodrome and next to an open-air cinema. Unfortunately, to secure this demi-paradise, a month's rent in advance had to be paid and I was the only one of the trio with any reserves of cash. Reminding them sadly that my allowances during my hospital imprisonment were gone with the wind, I watched them rushing out with glad cries and my cheque for £16. Oh well, anything to get out of that hotel.

The rest of the day I think. I think about the way you plan your life and the way you find yourself living it. I still think that if you really want, want with all your will-power and desire and determination, a way of life, you'll get it. But I don't know so cut-and-driedly what it is that I want, or perhaps nearer the truth, I want two

---

[16] Volunteer nurse.
[17] 1940s black singer who was reputed to have had an affair with Edwina Mountbatten.

different irreconcilable ways of life. I want freedom, I want to travel, I want to write. Since I first could form any plan of existence, those were the three things I sought after. Sometimes it comes over me in a wave so that I know I can't endure to die and not see all the places in the world still only names to me. Then there comes the complication of sex. To be logical I should be able to say marriage will interfere beyond adjustment with the way I want to live, therefore I must take love as it comes to me without tics and go free after that. But all my deepest instincts know that that way of life is shoddy and cheap and second-rate and unworthy of me. So here I am, torn between two ways of living, unable to see any compromise which will reconcile them.

4 April 1942

Well, eventually I escaped from that hospital and, having been given what I considered a pretty inadequate four days' sick leave, I went down to Alexandria with a WAAF called Pamela Sayers, who had been imprisoned in hospital at the same time as myself. Her husband is stationed at Abu Kebir, just outside Alexandria, and she invited me to spend my sick leave in the WAAF Mess there.

It was an enjoyable four days of walking from the bungalow through an English-reminding and homesick-bringing garden, to the beach and the Mediterranean. Of playing chess and getting better at it, of eating and drinking and laughing a lot in the Yugoslav Mess, of visiting

Pamela's flat, of exploring Alexandria, so much cleaner, cooler and less cramped than Cairo. And the last night I went on a party with Dulcie Stewart, whom I used to know in England and who is posted now to Abu Kebir, to see the nightlife of Alex. The men with us were pretty frightful and the evening the sort of thing that is only enjoyable if spent with people you like and then only fun very occasionally. We drank at the Cecil Hotel, we ate at the Union Club, we danced at the Monseigneur and the Excelsior until one o'clock and I got to bed at half past two.

Then there was the train journey back through the green and pleasant Delta valley and the unpacking and settling into our flat. I'm tired now and have to work tomorrow so I will describe the flat later.

10 April 1942

Life at the moment is very, very good and if only Alec were here with me it would be quite perfect, but perhaps in two or three weeks' time he will be able to come up and see me.

The flat is superb and I am living in the largest of the three bedrooms. It has a double bed and delightful green wood furniture. I have hung up my pictures, put out my books, unpacked all my possessions and am now hoping that the fourth flat sharer won't be wanted by Elizabeth and Diana, so that it can be my room permanently. Our servant is called Abdul, a small Egyptian who cooks and cleans and generally waits on us, and I find it still incredible that I am the part owner of a flat with no parental ties on it. We are almost at the entrance to the aerodrome and opposite the Heliopolis Sporting Club of which we have already been made members and to which I have once been.

So life outside work is good and life at work is good too. I am in a section I find most tremendously interesting. I am working with nice people and I have lots to do, so in that direction it is all utterly satisfactory. I expect soon I shall get to know people around the aerodrome and then there will be little left to ask of life.

I had the day off today and spent the morning exploring Heliopolis and doing some shopping. Then I got on the Metro and went over to Susan Perry's flat. She took me to lunch at the Gezira Club, first time I have seen it, and when she left me to go back on duty I made use of the place to the extent of taking an oh-so-welcome hot bath and writing a couple of letters, all this uneasily as I was not a member.

After I went into Cairo in a ghari,[18] into which an irresistible Arab child followed me and cleaned my shoes, and started my search for an Indian tailor, made somewhat difficult by the fact that I have simply no grip yet on the geography of Cairo and couldn't take a ghari as I didn't know where I wanted to go.

During my travels I discovered a shop where I bought two lengths of material for summer dresses and then stood outside the dress shop, absorbing ideas for getting them

[18] A horse-drawn carriage which was used as a taxi.

made up. Life out here is certainly less supplied with shop-made commodities than London but I am finding it fun – this doing things for yourself – and I am enjoying the fascination of Cairo: the dirty, colourful streets, the Arabs on the trams trying to sell you fly whisks and roses and trying to clean your shoes.

I found a tailor's in the end where an enormous woman and a posse of Arab stooges measured me for a gaberdine uniform. I nearly wept because they agreed to let me have it for 6½ and not 7½ guineas. My self-respect won't let me wear drill at night but unless my money comes through in a day or so from England, I am financially unstuck.

13 April 1942

Diana, Robbie and I are attending a week's course on Army Aerial Interpretation. Actually we think it is going to be of considerable help to us as we shall learn about desert warfare, which naturally wasn't touched on much in England, and we think we've a lot to learn from it. Unfortunately, however, the Army people giving it are embarrassingly humble and apologetic at having us on it and insist in addressing us always as 'you three experts', and asking us which of the lectures we won't bother to attend. All of which is highly flattering and would be most gratifying but for the fact that later on we hear we are to have tests and 'us three experts will of course head the list of marks'. We three experts don't at all share their confidence in our genius and feel that for the honour of the Air Force, of which we women are the sole representatives, cribs must be relied upon. Luckily Remington, with whom I work, possesses some, having done the course recently himself. We, as I have said, are the only Air Force. There's one naval officer who has made a great mistake in growing a beard, a couple of foreigners (Indian and Polish) and the rest are Army officers, one or two of whom time may reveal as pleasant enough. We sit at tables in a smallish room, drink tea at eleven and stop work at the wonderful hour of four.

Today after work Diana and I went riding, Diana having undertaken to teach me. It was the most wonderful afternoon I have spent in ages. We walked our horses out into a quiet corner of the desert and then Diana tied hers to a tree, produced a length of rope and an enormous whip and made me ride round her in circles. She said she was very pleased with my progress and I did so enjoy it, especially the ride back, when we passed Arabs who called out to us 'Saida', and Arab children who ran after our horses shouting for baksheesh.

19 April 1942

Letters from England are beginning to arrive. I've had one from Patsy Cunningham, an airgraph from Auntie Gertie and today there was a long newsy letter from Molly. No letters have arrived from Mother, which is peculiar, so I have sent her a cable today in case she's not receiving mine either.

It is getting hellishly hot here: yesterday it was 105°

in the shade and today seems equally stifling. This is my week to do the household catering and I had an embarrassing scene with Abdul this afternoon. For some time now Abdul has been complaining with, we feel, a certain justification that he is overworked, that he is a cook only and here he has to be suffragi – cook, batman, everything – and he has been trying to get us to hire his brother. Elizabeth, a more masterful personality than myself, has not encouraged the idea. But with me in uneasy control, Abdul has seen his moment. So this afternoon, brother was brought in and shown to me and I only managed to fob off his immediate commencement of work by saying I must consult with the others and that he must first bring his police working permit. What Elizabeth will say to this I do not like to think. Still I am getting more forceful in the east and I am bargaining with shopkeepers and ghari drivers and sporting a curt been-here-for-a-year, seen-it-all expression to Arabs wanting to show me the mosques and the bazaars.

Incidentally it is now over two weeks since I heard from Alec. Elizabeth has dismissed him to the ranks of insincerity with an 'Oh well, lots of men can't be bothered to write letters'.

22 April 1942

Yesterday evening and this morning were bad. There was the worry of Diana taken away to hospital with suspected, but thank God not, meningitis.

At lunchtime, walking to the Metro, I met Honor and

Stevie, fresh from England. They were full of their wonderful voyage and their not-yet-left-them-for-the-desert boyfriends. I remember myself a few weeks back at the hotel before Alec was posted, only it seems years ago and all unreal, and I was wretched.

Then coming in this afternoon there were four letters for me and one was his. He thinks he'll be coming to Heliopolis on 4 May to take our Army Interpretation course as he thinks he wangled it. My other letters were from the bank, Barbie and Bunty.

25 April 1942

In the middle of the course's last lecture – something for gunners on Morton's method of what sounded like 'griddling obliques' which really I had practically no grip on – Robbie said to me, 'You wouldn't like to come to a peculiar party tonight, would you?' Apparently one of the PRU pilots, just married, was giving a house-warming and all of PRU were going along to it. So I said I thought I'd like to, remembering that somewhere back in my past I had a creed that all experiences were ultimately worthwhile and none of them should be evaded.

Two of the PRU people collected us at Robbie's pension and took us along to the Continental where everybody was meeting, to be guided by their host to his flat. I had only met some of the PRU pilots before, my Egyptian career being divided almost entirely between hospital and Army courses, and wasn't particularly impressed by them, though one or two proved pleasant enough. There was one called Peter King with whom I spent most of the evening and who was even interesting. And there was a fair-haired boy[19] with whom I had a bicker on introduction as his greeting was the cocky, conceited creed of the average pilot. However, I think I was wrong about him, as later he apologised and he had a bewildered, lost, unhappy look almost all the time. And the others said he was all right.

We went in carloads to the flat, somewhere in Gezira by the Nile. Inside we were led almost immediately to a table so full of food of every variety no description can do it justice. And even after four months out of England I was impressed. We ate ourselves silly, we drank and we danced. An air raid, rare for Cairo, occurred in the middle of it but we were undisturbed, it was nothing to London and anyway this was not our city, the Egyptians certainly not our people. It wasn't our homes or our families suffering a possible extinction: the damaging of Cairo had left us quite unmoved.

I got home at about two, the CO of the unit bringing

---

[19] Adrian Warburton: born in 1918. The riddle of flying Ace Warburton's death was only solved in 2003 when his wrecked plane and body were recovered in Germany. His legendary role in the defence of Malta was made into a film, *The Malta Story*, starring Alec Guinness, where he reportedly fell in love with a civilian although already married to a barmaid. On 12 April 1944, he was the pilot of Lockheed F-5B photographic reconnaissance aircraft which took off to photograph targets in Germany. His plane was last seen 100 miles north of Munich. He failed to rendezvous at a USAAF airfield in Sardinia and was never seen again.

me and three of the pilots home in his car and distributing us to our various flats in Heliopolis. I quite enjoyed it, particularly my conversations with the pilot Peter King (one of those when slightly drunk and only the truth is uttered). He was railing bitterly against Army officers, pongos. I said as far as I was concerned I preferred them, operational pilots were no good to women, anyone with any sense soon learnt to lay off them. He was bitterly resentful that a WAAF should ever associate with the Army, the pilots he thought were the only people doing anything worthwhile in the war. I don't know about that but I do know that I have had all I ever want of the heady glamour of the operational pilot, with his restlessness and his charm, his lust for good times and drinks and parties, his heartbreaking elusiveness of spirit and his sudden death.

29 April 1942

Last Sunday I and a boy from the (interpretation) course called Hugh Rice spent the day exploring the pyramids. He called for me at the flat in a taxi he had hired for the day. We went to Mena House Hotel and sat there drinking orangeade on the porch and looking unimpressedly at the pyramids and later eating lunch and having to take ourselves most firmly in hand to do the necessary walking to the pyramids. We discovered that we had both dabbled in journalism pre-war and all the day, with all these wonders of the world and the banks of the Nile as background, we discussed books and plays and personal ambitions. He is an enormous young man of nearly twenty-five, stationed at the moment in Baghdad, with that rare and refreshing sense of reality that while respecting a woman, can still realise that to become adult she must have made, even though to a lesser degree, the mistakes and experiments that are accepted in a man.

We walked over the dirty, stony, rubbish-littered ground among the pyramids and the sphinx with the other tourists and considered the whole thing yet another of life's anticlimaxes.

Then we went in a taxi to see a couple more statues – the best thing was the crowds of gaily dressed, dirty and beautiful Arab girls who called compliments out to us in the hopes of getting baksheesh. And all the way we talked about all we'd done pre-war, I telling him about Shell and the *Lecture Recorder*,[20] to my brief success with *Eve's Journal*[21] and the short-lived River Theatre Company.[22] And then I told him about after the war, how I must travel and I must write and he asked how I was going to fit marriage into that. So I said that, until this was out of my system, I could never settle down. He asked how I knew I ever would get it out. Then I answered I must only hope I met someone who shared my ideas.

[20] A magazine, along the lines of *Reader's Digest*, on which I had an editing job.
[21] To which I sold my first poem.
[22] A group of semi-professional actors who performed on a barge and whom I helped in a fetch-and-carry capacity.

We had tea in the garden at Mena House and danced there and then he came back and had dinner at the flat with Diana and Elizabeth. They went out after to dance and we sat talking. I told him a bit about Red and he said it was probably a very good thing to happen. There are two reactions I had expected to Red's story, pity or anger, both exaggerating its importance and giving it the undeserved importance of a tragedy. His acceptance of it as a part of growing up was the most refreshing thing I had ever experienced. And then I told him about Alec and how I was fighting between the security he offered and my lust to be free, only there doesn't seem now to be much of a struggle. At the moment he is as unreal as Red is now.

Cairo[23] was a great success on the whole. The course was very well run, the hours were fairly human and there was a pleasant assortment of students. There were British, NZ and Australians, a Greek captain, a Fleet Air Arm Swordfish observer, a Sikh, and of course our three WAAFs.

The WAAFs lived at Hell House (Heliopolis House Hotel) which was a short tram ride from the school. We were astonished to find three of them sitting demurely in a row when we entered the lecture-room, but like all WAAFs (as I later discovered) they are quite

[23] Hugh Rice's diary begins here.

at ease in overwhelmingly male surroundings, and in this particular case they showed us all up by getting the first three places.

There were the three of them only on the course. Robbie: small, dark, rather an affected voice, thinks she's a WAAF before she's a woman. A photographer in peacetime, usually of what she calls 'filthy pictures' for Men Only and so on.

Next, Diana Orlebar. A great Air Force name, and all the family are mad keen on the RAF, so Diana had no difficulty in getting commissioned and sent overseas at the tender age of nineteen. A bit dumpy, and with lingering traces of the coltish stage, she is nonetheless a very pretty girl, particularly her large grey eyes, which make conquests for her which she can't really cope with. Elizabeth, a hearty type of about thirty (who mothers her and defies convention by living with her RAF boyfriend) dismissed her to me by saying, 'The poor child is dead sexually.' I don't think Elizabeth is in the least bit loose or promiscuous but she wears her sex life, defiantly, on her sleeve, which is not the best place.

Halfway through the course poor Diana was taken ill. Next day we were warned that there was a danger of CSM which in fact it turned out to be, though the crisis was passed and she was getting better before she really realised what was the matter.

Before she was taken ill, I had suggested to her one morning on the course that we made up a small party to go to the pyramids. She said that she couldn't manage either of the two days I suggested, so I guessed that it was her way of saying that I'd had it, and forgot all about it. So I was rather surprised, two days before the end of the course, when the third WAAF, Joan Bawden, waylaid me in a doorway and asked if the trip to the pyramids was still on. Was it on!

I want to get Joan exactly right in this diary – the right word all the time. I shan't succeed, but it doesn't perhaps matter much because I shan't need any reminders of Joan. Not that I have fallen – (like a number of my recently acquired female friends, she is practically engaged!) but just that she has been a wonderfully soothing and civilising influence.

She began to do me good the moment I walked into her flat and she enthusiastically showed me over it. Of course I was entranced – it was the first private house I had been in since Durban and the three of them have made a real home of it. Fortunately the furniture and decorations were a good starting point and they have added an atmosphere of their own. They take it in turns to do the housekeeping, and the cooking and chores are done by one Abdul, who seems, from the row that comes from the kitchen, to bring in most of his numerous family to help live at no extra charge.

We left for Mena in a taxi I had got for the day for thirty bob, which was pretty reasonable. Joan wore a green and flowered dress designed by her mother whose profession it is, and looked very cool and attractive. A lot of reddish-auburn hair (too much for WAAF regs!), widely-set light blue eyes, an attractive smile and a musical laugh is a description which reads rather ludicrously and in any case doesn't convey the picture – as I said I shouldn't be able to do; better left out. But on with story.

I kept the conversation on rather a stilted level as far as Mena – a fault of mine, desperately searching for subjects, which I change with a bewildering lack of logic at an unexpected moment. However, she soon knocked that nonsense out of me and at Mena House we had a couple of squashes on the terrace and planned the day.

The general attitude to the pyramids (we decided over a good lunch, in that nicest of all Egyptian hotels) was one of supercilious indifference to all the things tourists should do – guides, camels, tombs etc. We said we would just stroll over to the sphinx.

We wandered round the pyramids, which are only a couple of hundred yards from the hotel, and a few yards further from the Cairo trams terminus.

Then we went on to Memphis, a twenty-mile drive along a Nile canal, and there saw the Memphis Colossus: now laid low and somewhat battered, but a most impressive bit of work and worth the trip. And so back to Mena House, where we had tea on the lawn and danced in a delightful setting to a good band. Joan asked me back to their flat for dinner, so we returned to Cairo at about eight.

By the time we got back I knew Joan a good deal better. The story of Alec, of Red, her fighter-boy when she was Cpl Bawden, her home, her parents, convent *education, and all her troubles and ambitions – plenty of both.*

She seems to be very much in love with an AA gunner now in Suez whom she met on the ship coming out. Afraid of shipboard glamour, she was having a six-months try-out, expecting Alec to win the battle against her literary and travelling ambitions. She tries to look the thing in the face but I don't think she reaches a terribly realistic answer – though a far more practical one than I ever should in similar circumstances. To me, Alec I think must be too imaginative, cautious, and Victorian for Joan, who wants security without (at first) the stolidity which it would probably carry with it. This is really an infatuation of sorts – and I define infatuation as a state of mind in which a person can fill one part of one's life completely to the exclusion of all the others and not to the satisfaction of them all, which is the state of being in love.

Joan took this to be a suggestion on my part that the dominant side in her case is the physical, but I think she is also a little in love with being in love, even the unhappiness it is causing her. But that is probably unfair and misjudges the maturity of her outlook.

Anyway, I think it would be a mistake though I shall never say so – it's her problem. She wants someone who will help her get her many bugs out of her system before she settles down to life in a domesticated family circle – which she will do very well eventually. Also he is probably her intellectual inferior, apart from the advantage of age, and would tend to stifle her ambitions as a novelist, journalist and seeker of experience generally. Yet even were he inclined to support or foster that side of her life, it could only be a success were he able to lead her and help her and have her respect in those ways as well as a husband. Or so I think, but that is probably a very male point of view and a rather smug one too.

Of course I am rather flattered to have Joan as a confidante.

One of the reasons why I am a little suspicious of her powers of judgement in her own affairs as yet is that she hasn't seen through me to a greater extent than she has already! I suppose at least I am a better listener and a more restrained commentator than most, particularly her Cairo circle of WAAFs and pilots. And I am, no doubt, a better one because I am subconsciously anxious for mental (or spiritual? – I want a word) intimacy with someone – a sort of focus for a loneliness complex in one who is at once gregarious and yet forced into a good deal of emotional and social isolation from time to time, and forced to stand alone when the inclination is to lean, or at least have sympathetic understanding to fall back on.

But if it is sympathetic understanding that I am looking for in Joan, then my attitude to her is in part very hypocritical, selfish and rather degrading. (And I am probably too inhibited anyway to give her much chance of being sympathetically understanding!) On the other hand, all this introspection may be nonsense and my conclusions fake – I hope so. Then my attitude to Joan becomes much more creditable and my fear of being dishonest with her is removed. In fact everything is simplified enormously.

Now out here and for the last year or two generally, my adaptations have been all in the direction of the famous 'brutalising' process the Army caters for and some sincerity has gone by the board, or at least gotten buried pretty deep. But Joan, bless her, has dug it up and is constantly throwing it in my face, unknown to herself.

5 May 1942

I am ill again and in bed, only not so badly this time, and in the flat instead of hospital, thanks to the kind heart of the station MO who is horrified that women should have been sent here anyway and in particular women as young as me.

There has been a khamsin[24] in the last few days and the heat has been unbelievable: a sucking scorching furnace that dries all the cool air out of your body the moment you step outside into it. So by the time you have walked up the aerodrome perimeter track to PRU, if you're me you're already useless. Anyway, I've been sick and I've got a cold and I've started this wretched mysterious nightly temperature again and felt just too awful to describe. To add to my woes a few days ago the

[24] Tropical wind.

station surgical officer removed the base of my poisoned thumb nail. He did it very well with a local anaesthetic and even as abject a coward as I am couldn't complain that it hurt, but there seems to be some doubt now as to whether a new nail will ever grow. I hope I am eventually able to take this climate because the last thing I want to happen is to be returned home defeated by it.

Oh yes, Joyce Davidge has just arrived out here and is staying in the flat, in Diana's bedroom, until she's posted to her station. I was so very glad to see her about and I told her about my voyage out and she told me about hers and her boyfriend acquired en route, to our mutual satisfaction. And Alec, after all, hasn't come to Helio on that course though he has some hope that he may be able to get up here next Saturday.

27 May 1942

The things in my days. The return from hospital of Diana only she has to go back again today for a further examination.

The evening came around and Joyce and I lay in bed talking almost to dawn about Alec and about Nutty[25] and about the exhaustingness of Elizabeth.

And the next day when borrowing Father Blunt's car we drove with Diana and a picnic lunch out to the Delta Barrage through fields and villages and along by the Nile.

---

[25] Joyce's boyfriend.

At the barrage there were the most beautiful gardens and we ate our lunch on the green wonderful grass, surrounded by palm and flame trees with white strange and lovely birds flying over our heads against the blue sky.

I am on duty in the evenings this week. Robbie and I go down to the Mess, eat sandwiches and drink lime and lemon on the terrace, surrounded by the PRU pilots. I think I've made a hit with one of them called Fergie. He sat beside me yesterday and we talked about the trips he and Gerry Glaister[26] were to do the next day.

Late last night he came into the hut where we were getting to work on his sortie and said to me, 'I've brought you a souvenir from Cyprus, a bottle of brandy. It's in the Duty Pilot's hut at the moment.' I am wildly tempted to cultivate him and see a pleasant series of evenings for both of us.

1 June 1942

Emotionally and physically, life has been full these last days. There was a fat, delightful-looking letter from Alec which on opening proved to contain a letter written to him from Sheila: a young thing he took around immediately before leaving England and who has apparently a deep and embarrassing love for him, hitherto (so he says) unsuspected. She has written to him twenty-four times in the first seven weeks of his absence from England. As

[26] Gerry Glaister, DFC. 1915–2005. A distinguished wartime pilot who became a successful BBC writer and producer.

she's only just twenty and he's very, very fond of her, he is loathing the idea of having to hurt her by telling her about me. Well, at this point my brain put up a weak cry of 'now's your moment to think and consider and if you have any doubts halt and hesitate'. I have lots of doubts, I expect I shall always have, I seem incapable of consecutive emotion. But with my whole soul filled with rage and anger, reason and intellect had practically no hearing and had jealous pains for quite two days. Poor Alec and poor poor Joan, hopelessly in this unhappy mixture of emotions.

Then there was a day I went to the zoo with Joyce and Diana and the day five Italian prisoners and a German general, second in command of the German Afrika Korps, were brought in a Lockheed to Heliopolis and we all went out to take a shufty.[27]

The general was very old, very tired and very shaken and walked stiffly and emotionlessly to the car. I felt sorry for him but was surprised at the hatred in me for the rest of them, who we thought were all Germans.

Then there was yesterday, when I went with Robbie, Gerry and Fergie to another PRU party. I was monopolised heavily by Fergie, which did not altogether surprise me. He sat with me on the couch eating delicious food and taking down our hair in the reckless way one does after a couple of whiskies. At this time he was imploring me firmly not to marry and never to settle down, telling

[27] Air Force slang: take a look.

me I would never stick it and I was every sort of fool even to contemplate the idea.

After the party I brought him back to the flat and tried his brandy and with Diana we started a pretty heavy drinking session, which ended in Fergie swaying down the stairs and assuring me, as far as I can remember, that he was going out of my life which narked me but not for long as he reappeared quite heavily the next morning and seems like staying.

I have got to the stage now that I can only laugh at myself because really I am an exasperating woman, with this perpetual heart shilly-shallying.

8 June 1942

Yesterday morning Robbie, Richard Hay[28] and I went down again to the Musque[29] where I bought a carved wooden statue, highly indecent and very funny: the Arab's idea of a female English tourist – naked to the waist, camera round neck and an air of profound respectability. I also wanted to buy a carved mug but couldn't get them down to the price I was prepared to pay. However, I shall return another day and try again, I do so like the Musque.

Then Richard took us down to the part of ancient Cairo, through streets officially out of bounds to troops, to visit three mosques where overshoes were tied onto our feet before we were admitted.

[28] A fellow photographic interpreter.
[29] The name for the Bazaar quarters.

The mosques were very lovely: vivid stained-glass windows, mother-of-pearl inlay and painted ceilings. Outside in the streets again, followed by our inevitable posse of grubby and picturesque children, we got a ghari and returned to civilisation.

This evening was not so pleasant as we had to go on working till 4 a.m. and alas, I have irretrievably lost Fergie.

14 June 1942

I am inclined to think it's all over with Alec. In these last few days the last of Durban, all the ship's glamour has gone and I see him as a stranger, a not entirely sincere person. Well, anyways, if it is over it was a very lovely interlude from which I must now extract myself as gently as I can.

On Saturday evening the phone at PRU rang and it was Hugh Rice for me, down in Cairo for three days from the Levant. We were slack so I got off duty at eight and went with him to the Continental roof restaurant. It was one of the best places I've been to in Cairo, cool and dimly lit, with multicoloured fairy lights, with the dark star-crammed sky above. We sat in an alcove talking as we'd talked before of life and loving and journalism and the arts, and danced at intervals to the satisfactory band playing old memories like 'Begin the Beguine' and the latest hit in Cairo, though already in England before I left it, 'Sand in My Shoes'.

I like Hugh so very much. He is intelligent, clear-thinking and refreshingly unsentimental; at the same time he's kind and sincere, with unbelievably beautiful manners.

He came to lunch the next day and left saying that he hoped to get back again to Cairo; I hope too that he comes very much.

A casual phone call to Joan resulted in an evening off for her and a very pleasant dinner-dance on the roof of the Continental – with a monumental bill as a result of a few liqueurs at astronomical prices! Joan was still in a state of chaos over Alec but I think he's had it. We shall see.

Before we left I had a lunch date at Joan's flat. As usual a very good meal tastefully served and, touchingly, with a special sweet called mush-mush fool organised by Diana because I once said I liked it. Elizabeth was there, just back from a fortnight in Tel Aviv with her Dennis. Diana still very shocked and relations consequently not of the best. Diana has a noisy pom called Lula, which was presented to her by the devoted Abdul when she asked him to get her 'a large pale dog suitable for riding'!

To help her recovery (she is nearly better now) I sent her some roses. I afterwards found I got five dozen for my money so it must have looked very ostentatious!

26 June 1942

A period of rigid economy has set in. This has been six months of carefree expenditure, with little thought or care of the inevitable tomorrow which, along with a statement from my English bank saying I have an overdraft, has at last arrived. So I am saving half my pay in England against the end of the war and have decided too that I had better write to Shell and let them know I don't ever intend to go back to them. Since I'm breaking from one security I may as well be brave and break from the lot, for even if in moments of cowardice I see a future in which my wits and my writing fail me and I pass into a lonely and unemployed old age, I have realised now I cannot marry someone I don't fully love to escape it and equally I can't sit for ever avoiding its possibility in a job I loathe.

I'm planning again about my independent future, how I shall travel and write and get a job in Europe immediately post-war, where there are sure to be masses going. Life is going to be full and exciting and if it has already taught me that I shall not find complete happiness and peace until I can find that person I can love more dearly than myself, it has also taught me that I should find only misery if I took in its place any substitute.

I had a very pleasant hour this morning rattling over the aerodrome in the back of an open three-ton lorry, past Italian prisoners cheerfully building a road, to the rifle range where I had my first lesson in revolver shooting.

23 June 1942

The war news isn't any too cheery. Only three weeks ago everyone was saying 'through to Tripoli' and now we're wondering whether there will be German parachute attacks on the Alexandria road. And goodness knows when the Eighth Army is going to stop retreating.[30] HQ Middle East is in chaos and plans are being discussed, much to our rage and indignation, for the evacuation of the WAAFs to South Africa. Still, says she with the usual British ostrich-in-the-sand attitude, I don't suppose it will come to that. I hope not anyhow because I am finding life quite pleasant here at the moment.

Robbie had lunch yesterday with someone called Walter Taylor Young who is a friend of Hugh's and told Robbie that he was applying for Hugh to come to their unit as an ALO,[31] which would mean he'd be stationed on the Canal and would be into Cairo frequently. I found the thought of that happening made me happy and excited for all of the evening but I sat firmly on my exuberance, having no trust at all now in the reliability or the durability of my emotions. And I must be careful too not to hurt Hugh. Robbie says I go through people like a tank and I've no realisation at all of what they suffer because of me. That isn't entirely true. If I let myself come out of

[30] The British Army was retreating from the Germans across the desert, towards Cairo.
[31] Air liaison officer.

my wall of self-protection I feel only too thoroughly all
their pain.

28 June 1942

The news gets worse. The German Army is past Mersa
Matruh and is still advancing. The German Radio has
announced that they will be in Alexandria by 5 July and
in Cairo by the 8th. We apparently intend to try and hold
them at the Qattara Pass. Nobody here seems to know
anything about anything. Certainly no one seems to have
any plans of action and we can only trust that those more
exalted than ourselves have a better grip than us on the
situation.

The PRU desert flight is back and the advanced air
headquarters is humiliatingly near Alexandria. The wogs
are getting into a fine panic about the prospect of air
raids. If we don't hold them at that Pass I suppose PRU
will remove itself to Palestine and I only pray to God that
they will let us go with them and not send us uselessly
to South Africa.

Alec came up this weekend; his people at Suez having
not apparently heard about the cancellation of all leave.
It wasn't a very happy weekend for either of us.

1 July 1942

I am writing this from an RAF station called, I
think, Ramallah – anyway just outside Jerusalem, having
joined that large group of people who from time to time

in this war have had to leave hurriedly before the Hun.[32]

The morning was fairly normal until we were told to burn anything we didn't want, go back and pack and be up again at the station by two o'clock. Hardly had I started my packing when Honor Clements came in at 12.45 and said we must have everything packed and be ready to leave by plane for Lydda at two o'clock.

We threw clothes into cases, bolted bits of food, paid a weeping Abdul and Hamed. We had to leave sadly so many of our clothes and, with what we could take packed with us into a lorry, drove down to the aerodrome with Flight Lieutenant Stephenson.

The WAAFs were being flown away a few at a time in the unit's two Beaufighters. I went in one with Margaret Perkins and Diana, clambering in and crouching uncomfortably among our luggage in the rear. Warby,[33] the blond, beautiful unit's Ace was our pilot. We took off and flew over Ismailiya, the Canal, the desert and along the coast by the sea to Lydda. It was a wonderful trip. I stood up in the back looking at the beauty of the clouds and thought – this is living.

At Lydda he returned to bring up more of us and we went into the Mess to drink tea and eat sandwiches and then to be taken in an open lorry to this place, Ramallah, where we are to spend at least the night.

What I have seen of Palestine I like. It's green and

---

[32] Having fought across Libya and Egypt, Rommel's Afrika Korps had this day reached the final British defences at El Alamein.
[33] Adrian Warburton.

comparatively cool and so much more like England than Cairo. Part of me is loving all this adventure with a most unworthy zest; however, the adventure has had, I must say, a slight setback. On my way to wash in a bathroom just filled with those enormous horror-filling cockroaches I fell over a case in the darkness and cut my shin agonisingly.

Heard the good news (in a way!) that the PRO WAAFs have been evacuated to Raule – Joan rang up in a state of high excitement. Had a mildly embarrassing phone conversation in the Mess and fixed a provisional date for the following Sunday.

4 July 1942

The last two days have been excitement saturated. The second day of our arrival Diana and I, with an RAF type we found in the Mess called Michael Dallas, took ourselves by taxi to Tel Aviv: a somewhat shoddy little seaside town, appearing to be almost entirely populated by German Jews.

We met an ALO called Peter Oxele, a friend of Michael's, and sat in a café by the shore drinking iced coffee, eating strawberries and cream and laughing a lot.

Then we went on to the bar of a hotel called the Gatz Rimon, where we sat on high stools drinking shandies while a pianist played all our dear tunes, like 'Fools Rush In' and 'Begin the Beguine'.

Yesterday Diana, Robbie and I got a lift into Jerusalem, driving at a hectic speed along a hair-bend road, through scenery doubly beautiful after the deserts of Egypt.

Jerusalem is smaller and cleaner than Cairo but less impressive as a city. In the King David Hotel we met two of our unit and discovered from them that Hugh Rice is just outside Jerusalem and I am waiting now for him to phone me with the hope that we'll be able to meet some place, some time soon. We drank with Michael, another RAF officer, two pretty dreary Army jobs and Robbie, until after two in the King David, after which we ate a super colossal meal at a restaurant called Hess's. And then happily leaving the Army, we went on to explore the old city. After that we went back to a hotel called Princes where we drank until it was time to return.

The old city is a thousand times more fascinating than the Musque, having less of its catering-for-tourists atmosphere and I want to go back again often.

In the evening Diana and I sat talking in the Mess to two pleasant young pilots who are taking us to swim tomorrow at the Jaffa Club.

As far as the work or how the war goes, life is not so satisfactory. The news from Egypt continues to be grave but not hopeless and our orders become nothing more definite than to stay here until further instruction, which means sleeping somewhat sordidly on a mattress on the floor in a very dirty married quarter and having an indefinite holiday: this is an odd war.

7 July 1942

There was a Sunday with bathing at the Jaffa Club and drinking and eating at the Gatz Rimon and dancing later at one of the Tel Aviv nightclubs with two pilots from the Mess.

And then there was yesterday. There have been happy days in my life, very happy ones, but never one that touched the rapture of yesterday.

I drove into Jerusalem on a lorry with three of my co-WAAFs to meet Hugh, as arranged, in the King David bar. I thought – tomorrow will come with Alec and the mess I've made of his and my life and all the doubts and uncertainties, torment and indecision of these last months returning intensified so I said I will have this day perfect and it will be mine always afterwards, whatever after happens to me.

We drank in the King David; we had lunch in Queens and then Hugh said would I like to go to the Dead Sea.

We drove down in a taxi to 1200 feet below sea level and got out to drink lemonade in a café by the shore which might have been a setting for almost any Marlene Dietrich film, with sinister music faintly in the background and the odd desperate-looking character leaning by the counter and at the tables. We talked about books and films and ourselves and we walked for a way along the shore of the Dead Sea so that I could taste for myself its saltiness.

Then we rode through Jericho to the Transjordan frontier where we got out and walked across so that I could be able to say I'd been in Transjordan, the Jordan incidentally being a disappointingly muddy little stream.

We drove back to the King David where I washed and tidied and waited for Hugh's return from letter signing at Air Headquarters.

We drank again in the King David, laughing and talking with an ease and understanding I cannot dare hope can last. There seems to be nothing on which we don't meet and feel the same.

We had dinner back at the Queens where a perfect band played the 'Skaters Waltz' and 'Tales from the Vienna Woods', before reaching the more general dance tunes as the evening lengthened.

We ate lobster and apricot ices and danced a little and talked a lot, there is always so much to say to him. And we drove back down the Jerusalem road in his truck, I sitting beside him wrapped in a rug watching the stars and the night, my hair torn back by the wind. And then I was in bed and it was all over and reality is back again, although slightly glorified by the fact that he stayed the night here at Ramallah and is having tea in the garden with Diana and me after lunch. I am sitting on it hard, I am doing all I can to suppress it all and using every weapon against it of reason and experience. But underneath it all my heart is singing wildly and madly with joy refusing to be impressed by the mess and the complications. Here he is come at last – and he has never so much as held my hand.

Joan looked marvellous with sea water hair and Tei Aviv sunburn on her face. I hoped it wouldn't take too long to catch up lost ground. We fed on an omelet and shandy at Queens and Joan's enthusiasm was very warming as always. We decided to go to Jericho for the afternoon, and I negotiated a taxi at a pound and a quarter for the trip. Then off to Kallia, with Joan beside me. The run down she enjoyed, and decided the tawdry lido-café had an exciting atmosphere, rather South American, as she sipped her grapefruit, sitting bolt upright with wide eyes, like an expectant puppy. Diana called her a squirrel, which made her livid. We walked a couple of hundred yards along the beach past the BDAC base, and tasted the water just to see how salty it really was.

Then we went on to Jericho, so that Joan could say she'd seen Jordan and get a line to shoot about Transjordan itself.

The taxi driver was getting a bit reluctant by this time, so we went back to Jerusalem and as always I found when we got back that I knew Joan better than before but was ever more aware of how much more there is to know!

9 July 1942

Hugh had tea with us that afternoon in the garden but Diana and Harry were with us and our special selves, which we show only when together and alone, hid themselves between the surfaces of a nice, shy, large, young man and a not-very-talkative girl. He went away promising to arrange a trip with him to Haifa for Diana and me but I have since had a message from him that he has a poisoned heel and the trip has been briefly postponed.

So yesterday with Robbie, Margaret and Betty Harvey I went to Jaffa for a picnic lunch and a swim. We had our lunch made up at a café on the cliffs and walked up the beach till we found what looked a good spot to bathe. Camels in processions passed us on the lower firm sands; the sea was brilliant blue with white breakers; the sun and the sand were hot. I bathed, I ate lunch, I sat on the beach eating corn on the cob bought from an Arab, and thinking – this is the way to live.

Then, before going back, we thought we would bathe again. For a time we enjoyed ourselves, letting the waves beat upon us and carry us unsuspectingly out with their each retreat. Suddenly Robbie said to me, 'You'd better come in a bit, Joan, you're a long way out.' I started to swim but made no progress. She held her hand out to me but I could not reach it. I was tired and swimming only weakly against the suddenly ferocious waves. And then I got cramp in the sole of my foot. Robbie came out to me and tried to tow me in, both of us swimming on our backs but our progress was negligible, the waves separated us. I had then, looking at her white, tired face, an instance of terror such as I had never known in all my life before. I thought we would never reach the shore, I knew we would drown.

Another wave came over me, I swallowed water gasp-

241

ingly. In the distance I could see Margaret running across the beach to the nearest hut and lifebelts. I wanted so much to live, even with the present muddle it seems so tragic and wasteful to die like that. Terrified into strength, we fought silently and then regained water within our depth. We struggled to the shore as men arrived with lifebelts. It was a horrible experience and only Robbie's shovings and pushings at me as each shore-going wave broke over us got me back. I had doubts that in such a situation I would show the courage she did.

11 July 1942

Hugh came over at nine yesterday morning in his truck with an RAF medical officer called Michael Gallagher, to take me to Haifa. I sat in the front with the driver. After Egypt I shall never cease to enjoy the sight of grass and trees – it's a lovely country, Palestine.

Arriving at the Windsor Hotel, Hugh went off to work and the MO and I went to shop in the town, which is white and new and like Tel Aviv, until we met at Pross's for lunch.

After lunch, Hugh's not very strenuous work being ended, we drove in a taxi to see the view at the top of Mount Carmel, across the harbour and the bay to the borders of Syria. Then, having dropped the MO in the town, we went on to a beach to bathe. It was a perfect day, the clouds keeping off any burning heat, and we lay all afternoon on the sand, sleeping a little and talking with even greater ease and understanding. He is the one person in all my life with whom I have never had to pretend, from the very beginning with him I have been honest and the relief and joy and the content to be able to be without pretence and still be understood.

Later in the evening we bathed, playing unenergetically about in the warm waves and not until eight o'clock were we ready to leave, sitting waiting for the bus, both saturated in contentment.

We met Michael at the Casei, the nightclub on the front, where we dined.

It had a glass floor, a good band and paintings of London – Piccadilly, Marble Arch and Oxford Street – around the walls. The dance hostesses were painted and unalluring and fascinating to watch. It was sufficiently sordid to have an atmosphere of attraction and interest. I like these Palestinian nightclubs, they're all such good settings for dramatic scenes in novels or pictures I'd like to paint.

We had to leave at 10.30 in the middle of the cabarets because the driver was waiting to take us to Ramallah and Jerusalem. This time I sat with Hugh in the back on a pile of rugs and another round me, dozing comfortably in his arms. I knew without surprise or doubt that this at last was what I had always been seeking.

To Haifa Gallagher, our rather wild young Irish MO, asked if he could come, and I thought he would take a bit of the strain off me by pairing off with Diana. But when we got to Raule at nine o'clock, Diana, unlucky

243

as ever, was due to go on duty in the Ops Room – a duty which had fallen to her because Diana Neil, the arch flint of the outfit, had gone off to Beyrouth for a couple of days. So we went off as a threesome – Burger[34] and Joan in front, the doc and I in the back nobly taking all the bumps and being rewarded by the smirks of all we passed. We reached Haifa at eleven, with Joan enthusing about the trip up but doc and I rather sore.

I went off to the airport to try and locate 451 and a few other people, having left the other two at the Windsor for a coffee to be followed by a shopping expedition. After wrestling with the telephone service for some two hours I got back to our lunchtime rendez-vous at Pross's in time to buy Joan her inevitable shandy. Then a good meal, as always there, with the doc making his usual remarks on the edge of good taste, in spite of my previously delivered warnings that Joan was 'not his usual type'! Then a taxi up Carmel, to see the view and find a grassy patch to doze on, but we couldn't find a sufficiently unspoilt place so we decided to go down to the beach. At this stage the doc decided to go and visit some friends he knew in Haifa. At the time I thought he was being tactful, but later found out that he had a Russian girl in the town so his motives were not quite so altruistic as at first appeared.

---

[34] Hugh's driver.

Joan and I went on down the coast, at enormous expense, in this taxi, until we reached a very nice stretch of sand complete with dressing rooms. We lay on the beach and toasted until about six o'clock, getting drowsy and talkative by turns, I continuing the blessed process of getting to know Joan better, and both of us verging on little intimacies of understanding which made the afternoon another oasis of peaceful relaxation from the usual jolting routine. At half past six when the breeze was freshening we had a grand bathe in large breakers, which woke us up properly and gave us enormous appetites. After dressing we waited half an hour for a bus back to town and joined the doc an hour later than the appointed time: at the Casino, Joan being anxious to see something of the sordid side of Haifa nightlife!

She was not impressed by the hostesses in the least, though she blushed rather nicely when the doc described one of the more outrageous ones as 'sexy'. Mostly from fear of where the conversation might lead, I think!

We had a rather poor meal of Wiener Schnitzel, but we were more appreciative of quantity than quality after our afternoon in the open air, so it went down very well. The cabaret was above average. An excellent conjuror who called himself the 'Mexican Aristocrat', and the inevitable 'Chocolate Boys', whom I have now seen in every cabaret in the Middle East I should think (Live!).

At 10.15 the faithful Burger came to collect us. Joan

was dragged reluctantly from the cabaret, of which we had only seen half, and we set about getting as comfortable as we could for the long journey home. Doc got in front with Burger, Joan and I attempted to get comfortable in the back by spreading blankets over a tent which we had packed up in the back. We tried several torturous positions – not what the doc was sure was under way, but to give Joan a chance to sleep. We finally got settled down, Joan in my arms half on me and half on the tent, swathed in blankets and asleep on my shoulder. She woke when we went over the worst bumps, rubbed her eyes in a most attractive way, brushed back her hair and asked how uncomfortable I was. I was thoroughly enjoying the acute discomfort – arms aching, bottom paralysed and an iron rod gouging at my back! Occasionally I would be vastly embarrassed by the headlights of an overtaking car and prayed that it wasn't a staff car or the AOC!

We got to Raule at 1.30 a.m. and I had a job shaking Joan to wake her up enough to clamber out of the lorry. She said a dazed goodnight, slipped into her quarters and woke up Elizabeth as she was getting to bed – with bad consequences for her reputation!

18 July 1942

Yesterday morning we were told that on the day after six of us were to be returned to Helio on Cloudy Jane, the unit's Lockheed Electra, and the remaining five the day after that.[35] So Diana and I went for a farewell visit to Jerusalem, riding in on a duty run lorry. It's a super run into Jerusalem and we tore along the twisting road at an unbelievable speed.

At the King David we phoned Hugh's office, to invite him out to a farewell lunch, but alas he was still away on his Beirut expedition. So we found an Elizabeth Arden salon and slipped within for three hours, having the traces of three weeks' country life removed from our faces, hair and hands. A Hungarian did my hair, an Austrian my nails and another Austrian, trained in America, gave me a facial. It was the first time I had ever had that done and found at any rate the first part of it a most painful process. When we ultimately emerged we were cleaner and, we hoped, more glamorous.

In the evening Hugh phoned saying that he too might be coming down to Helio on business for the day and would take me out to dinner if he did. He sounded pretty definite then but he should have arrived by now and I'm losing hope as it gets later. Still he said if he didn't manage today he'd be coming the week after.

The next morning we packed ourselves and our luggage into a lorry and drove over to Lydda Airport to be transferred into Cloudy Jane and arrived back at Helio just before lunch. I am getting somewhat blasé now about travelling places by air and dozed most of the way back.

---

[35] We had been unable to continue our interpretation work in Palestine and with successful British counter-attacks having held up the German advance it was now considered necessary that we return.

247

We had lunch in the Mess and then, as our flat had been sold in our absence, moved once again, if only temporarily, into Hell House. It is four months since we were here before. So here we are back again in unlovable Egypt and starting work once more tomorrow afternoon.

Letter to Joan filed in diary

Sunday

Dear Joan,

Owing to pressure of work I have had a telephone put in my tent, so you can now make operational calls without fear of sabotage at this end. But please ask for ALO, otherwise the call will go to the Mess.

I hope you weren't too exhausted the morning after we got back from Haifa. You'll probably be amused to hear my driver's comment to the doc on the way home: 'Captain's having a good time tonight sir – she's a nice little thing; didn't do so bad myself on the way up!' You might let me know what disciplinary action you'd like me to take. His day off is Saturday.

We got back here at 3.30 a.m. – a natural result of the doc remembering a short cut. We climbed a mountain road for centuries, ears popping, and came out in an Arab village perched on a hill-top with cloud all around. The only human being we could dig out was too drunk to stand, and the driver by this time was a corpse in the back – my only link with reality was the smell of 4711 or Black Mischief or

something, which clung to my shirt and fortified me
until we hit the right road. I suppose I shall have to
get it washed eventually!
  Yours,
  Hugh

20 July 1942

Hugh arrived yesterday morning, having had to spend the night at Suez, and turned up to have tea with me in Hell House, walking up with me to the aerodrome after as he had to see Roger about some work. Roger wasn't available so he had an excuse for not returning immediately to Palestine and collected me at eleven the next morning.

We had a drink in the Continental and talked again with all that pleasure we find in every subject before going to a bookshop where I bought a copy of *For Whom the Bell Tolls*, which I have lent to Hugh and which I want to read and reread as one of the best modern novels I have ever read.

We went back to the Continental for a last drink before going to Gezira for lunch, which we ate on the terrace, laughing a lot. I am always so happy with Hugh, the past and the future never matter and I never seem to worry or doubt when he's with me that everything won't ultimately be all right.

After lunch we walked over the Gezira golf course and lay down under a willow tree to talk and laugh. Hugh had his arm in a sling from an accident in his truck and we decided no one would admonish anyone with such an impressive-seeming desert war wound.

All too soon it was four o'clock and I had to be getting back to work and we both discovered we had this same sense of fleeting time robbing us remorselessly of our happiest hours and making them so soon the unreal past. He knows now that I am ending things with Alec.

Broke because it was Sunday, I was forced to be very economical until the bank opened the next day. So I lunched alone at Jimmy's, made a number of phone calls to try and locate Peter, and finally called up Joan, whom I dragged from bed at Hell House so that she sounded very cross by the time she reached the phone – I was invited to tea but I went very apprehensively until her delighted smile, as ever, reassured me.

Next day, arrived late at Hell House to meet Joan, and found her on the terrace drinking lime with Robbie. We took a taxi to the Continental and had a couple of drinks before going out to do a bit of bookshop brows-ing. Joan looked marvellous – I must be getting in deep. I shocked myself by feeling immensely relieved when she told me, half defiantly, that Alec has definitely had it. I wonder if he has.

Joan bought For Whom the Bell Tolls, *the new Hemingway, and forthwith lent it to me to read as she has already read it. I think it a masterpiece – and I shall be very interested to discuss it with Joan and hear why it impressed her so much.*

We had a good lunch at Gezira, and then wandered round the golf course in search of seclusion, eventually finding it under the shade of a willow by the cricket ground, where there was shade and quiet and plenty of long grass to suck. We said little but what we said was, to me, heavy with meaning. It was a marvellous two hours but it left me in a turmoil. I suppose I shall get it sorted out.

24 July 1942

Hugh left in the afternoon the next day, leaving a message for me with Tony Bridge that he'd be down again in a fortnight and would phone me up.

He came round to lunch at our new pension with Tony but I was out pursuing my lost luggage, successfully, at an aerodrome where we were entertained delightfully by the Station's young and alluring wing commander and his satellites.

My other news is that Diana and I are now living in Holly Lodge Pension, in a large pleasantly furnished room with a balcony, excellent food and service and that enchanting Tony Bridge from the course for company. We think we're going to like it here a lot and it's certainly a lot less trouble than a flat.

I've had a letter from Alec saying that he thinks it's pretty obvious that I've changed my mind, arriving the same day that I wrote to tell him that I had. So that's pretty well the end of that. To say I'm sorry I hurt him is pretty inadequate to describe how I feel about it but I am only thankful that I was able to realise my mistake so soon and to save ourselves from more of that misery and each-other-hurting which we were just beginning on. It's been an experience which in its early days was wonderfully happy but which for its latter part I shall never cease to be sorry for.

I beat it to Joan's pension to try and see her for a final lunch. She and Diana were looking for lost luggage. However, it was probably an absolute act of God that I missed Joan, for I was still in a whirl after our day out the previous day, and I should probably have said something very rash, whereas all this has got to be very carefully thought, both as to my own position, and, having decided on it, what is to be taken to Joan.

Next time I see her I'll hold everything and see how I feel. She mustn't be played around with under any circumstances. But someone's going to be very very lucky. I'm afraid it won't be me, and ever more afraid that it oughtn't to be, even if it could.

29 July 1942

Last night we had fun. Robbie and Polly[36] came to dinner with us and Tony at the pension and during the

---

[36] Robbie's boyfriend who proposed to her later and then pulled out before their wedding day.

afternoon Peter Irksel, whom we met that first afternoon in Tel Aviv, phoned me up to take me out so I asked him along to join the party.

After dinner we left Robbie and Polly, who are in love, contented with their lot the sofa and four of us took a taxi to the Continental roof garden where we ate ices, drank coffees, danced, watched the cabaret and laughed a lot. Then we took two gharis and drove to the English Bridge, Peter and I sitting up on the box and driving ours ourselves, fairly tearing down the moonlit streets and passing Tony and Diana dangerously and excitingly at a bend in the road. At the English Bridge we took a felucca and sailed for an hour on the Nile. The moon was full and beautiful, there was a breeze and a lot of stars. It was quite, quite lovely and against the banks were the high arched masts of moored feluccas, black against blue. I thought – if it were only Hugh with me it would be perfect and I expect Tony was wishing instead of us he had his wife. Still the night was gay and we got to bed eventually at half past two.

30 July 1942

In the middle of the night I was woken up by the sirens: Cairo's heaviest raid was on. It was a superb moonlight night and they were dive-bombing Helio aerodrome. Diana and I watched it from our bedroom window, saw the searchlights and the gun flashes, heard the aircraft, the guns, the bombs and after it all the gentle patter of the shrapnel falling on the streets and gardens. It was not a bad raid by London standards but it was the first of such size to happen here.

In the morning Tony Bridge called up to us from the garden an account of the damage and we gathered from his description that rivers of blood and petrol would greet us as we entered the aerodrome. The damage was, in fact, quite considerable. Two hangars were gutted, several buildings destroyed, a few aircraft pranged, including the rendering unserviceable of all the unit Spitfires except one, thanks to the aerodrome's criminally stupid habit of never attempting to disperse them. There ought to be a terrific stink about it and a blitz of gigantic proportions of the Station CO or whoever was responsible. It isn't as if we've got so many Spitfires out here either.

Our huts were knocked about a bit and as a result of it all we are moving today to our new offices off the aerodrome buildings instead of waiting a month for them to be got ready for us. Happily, it's almost next door to our pension so we've been able to have the extra half-hour in bed.

Chalked up on the back of a long convoy – 'Please pass quietly – driver asleep'. After two days' flat-hunting we have found a very good flat. Five minutes' walk from the King David, four bedrooms, dining and drawing rooms, kitchen, bathroom, refrigerator, electric toaster and all the rest.

There have been two consecutive raids on Helio, but the gen came through quickly both times with details of casualties (which were very light) so I didn't have much chance to worry about Joan. Should I worry about Joan? Do I really worry about Joan? Find out, I suppose, on Friday. Hope so!

19 August 1942

I have left this for far too long unwritten through the most eventful days of my life.

Last Friday week at lunchtime Hugh phoned up and arranged to call for me at seven that evening. I went back to a lunch I couldn't eat, trying to control my voice and my hands.

We went out to Mena House, eating our meal by the swimming pool and talking, our last time uninvolved, with each other, asking each other (now that we were free) for the truth under a surface order of conventional words. I told him that I had ended things finally with Alec. I told him the whole of that story as fully as I could. Then we drove back to the Continental. In the taxi I think he made his last fight of sensibleness against this strange, strong, unbelievable thing. For himself, he said, he was prepared to take any risks but he hesitated when they involved other people.

We drank orangeade at the Continental and talked more lightly, laughing a little. Outside he bought me roses and ropes of jasmine. In the second taxi going home I knew that the time had come; things could stay no longer as they were. The atmosphere was taut. Suddenly I knew what I wanted to do, what was right to do and I took his hand. All of it came out then, the unbelievable yet inevitable miracle that he had loved me from that very first day and more each time, but like me he had tried to kill it and force it under, but it had got to the stage when he could have stood no more.

The taxi drove us past my pension, when finally we redirected him and got to my door. There was nothing we could say. It was a daze of glory. He walked all the way back from Heliopolis to Cairo, to try and get it straight in his mind. I think I slept about two hours that night.

We had lunch together the next day but our decision had been made for us by the war. He was posted permanently into the desert on a job he'd always been wanting to do. It would possibly be three months before he could get up to see me again so we said it would satisfy even our reason if by the end of that time the glory was still there, and we had all of the last day together from lunchtime until that night.

We had lunch at Gezira and tea by the pool. We drank and dined at the Continental and never has anything been more perfect. There was simply nothing I could say; for once Hugh did most of the talking.

Then we drove to the English Bridge in a ghari and went on the Nile. It was two I think when he finally left me. I cried for a few minutes angrily, without expectation of comfort, against the pension door as I heard his taxi go away but then this is all any of us have these days and really I had been so very lucky. And the wonderful thing is that he has been recommended for a staff course in

November, which means if it comes off he'll be out of the desert, but November is a long time and any day now the expected blow-up in the desert will begin. It means nothing now except that he might be killed or captured or I might again be permanently evacuated so that we'll be separated for all of this endless war. Still I have had a lot already, a glimpse of something some people never get. Since he's gone I've had one letter and some flowers with a wonderful note on my birthday. There may be another letter today.

26 August 1942

In his last letter Hugh had said he might be up one day this week to collect his kit. On Sunday Tony Bridge took me out to lunch at Hell House and on returning, mellowed by gin and lime and beer and brandy, I was en route to sleep when they said, 'Someone's been phoning you from the Continental, about four times in the last hour.' I knew at once it was Hugh. I phoned the Continental and he said he'd be right round. I made Tony sit in the lounge with me and talk to me because I had somehow to control myself and take some sort of grip again. I didn't much like this being in such a state about him when before we'd been such easy friends.

At last he came and we talked until tea with Tony and Diana. He had to go at five but returned to collect me for the evening at eight.

We went again to the Continental and by that time both of us had got over this strangeness. We were friends again as well as being in love. We discussed our future a little, deciding that by December we would know without doubt and go straight ahead. We danced a little, then there was an air raid and we got tired of sitting on the lightless roof so returned to Heliopolis where, with the All Clear, we danced for a little at Hell House.

Then we came back to the pension to make love lightly and laugh a lot. He was going to phone me in the morning to say if he had to go back that day or not.

He didn't and I was walking back to the pension when he came up in the street beside me. He was returning at three that day so I changed and returned to Hell House for lunch.

I don't know when I'll see him again. He hoped to come this weekend but I think myself the desert business will have started before then. Still, once his letters start coming I shan't mind so much, as he said the war must be halfway over and we are both so young. We are so lucky and we will be very very happy.

15 December 1942

I doubt if I shall continue this, but in ending a diary that has followed continuously my life from the outbreak of war until this point three years later, I owe it I feel a summary at least of my situation today.

Hugh and I got engaged in October and hope to be married in January. I am still in Cairo living in a flat with a WAAF called Jean Mitchell. Hugh is in the desert and I have seen him only several times for a few days during the last four months. But somehow, unwise, young, stupid, selfish, bewildered and unguided, I have achieved a goal I only dimly realised I was seeking. There are many events in the last three years I regret but I think because of them I stand today on the edges of adulthood and a way of living I wanted in my heart.

Events of 1942

20 January At the Wannsee Conference, top-ranking Nazis coordinated the 'Final Solution'.

21 January Rommel launched a fresh offensive in Africa, which would come within sixty miles of the Allied base at Alexandria.

31 May The British government stepped up the bombing campaign, launching the war's first 1000-bomber raid against Cologne.

21 June Rommel reached the Egyptian border, taking the Libyan port of Tobruk and capturing over 35,000 British troops.

1 July Rommel was halted at the British defensive positions at El Alamein, 150 miles from Cairo.

13 August General Montgomery assumed command of the Eighth Army.

22 August Germany launched the assault on Stalingrad, initiating one of the bloodiest battles of the war.

3 November Montgomery led the Allies to victory over Rommel at El Alamein, forcing Axis troops to retreat from North Africa.

AFTERWORD

I read my grandmother's diaries for the first time about two years ago. She had kept them stacked away for over fifty years before letting anyone in the family read them. This was not because they contained wartime secrets (which, in fact, they did: hers), or because the memory of it was too painful, but because no-one had asked to see them before. I read the whole lot in one sitting.

As soon as I started to read I realised that the twenty-something girl in her swanky new uniform, desperate for adventure, was very much the same character as the eighty-year-old woman who had taught me to play Rummy aged six. I couldn't get the diaries out of my head so, with her permission, passed them on to my literary agent, Claire Paterson, with a note saying some-thing like 'I'm sure you dread getting handed anything written by people's relatives.' I was delighted and not really at all surprised when Claire called me on a Monday morning after a weekend, she claimed, in which she had not been able to drag herself away from my grand-mother's adventures. She wanted to meet her, and she was convinced that the diaries would have interest from publishers. In the meantime, they were passed around Claire's office where they were greeted with universal enthusiasm. One morning I took a photograph of my grandmother on her wedding day into the office. 'Oooh! Is that Joan?' demanded Molly and Rebecca from opposite ends of the room, practically trampling over each other to take a look at her picture. They wanted to put a face to what they had read. I was lucky enough to have that with me already.

What makes these diaries remarkable is that the writer isn't a cabinet minister, or a spy, or a previously unknown confident of Churchill. She is a very normal 19 year-old from Claygate, who happened to live through the most extraordinary years of twentieth century. When I spoke to my grandmother about what she had written, she said that she couldn't believe how much time she had spent talking about boys and parties, considering what was going on in the world around her. I said that those were the bits I liked the most. It was comforting, and hilarious and *important*, I felt, to know that even during the war, girls were worrying about how they looked when boys – or, rather, airmen – talked to them or where the next dance would be. This was the startling thing about the diaries – how like mine they were! For my generation, it is difficult to imagine what living through the war was like, yet somehow I feel that I learned more about it through these diaries than I could have done through any number of documentaries, or museums, or artefacts, or biographies. I had always pictured women during the war 'getting on with it back home', living a sober existence in black and white. When I had finished the diaries, the young girls she wrote of seemed to dance off the pages, in all colours.

Through her writing, those strange years came alive for me. I found it just as atmospheric to read of the days when nothing much happened – when it seemed important to record how much cleaning and tidying up had been done – as I did to read about the urgency of the war, when living for the moment was all anyone felt they had time for. Somehow, these diaries explain that conundrum: how 'normal' life was suddenly rendered banal, whilst the banal was raised up to the sacred. In these diaries, a good supper takes on as much importance as the air raids. And like my first term at university, a great deal of my grandmother's time at the start of the war was spent sitting around and waiting for something to happen. I found this oddly comforting.

These diaries are one woman's journey – a woman who left those years far behind her and who went on to become a mother, a grandmother and a great-grandmother. I suppose what I felt most of all when I came to the last page was gratitude. I wanted to thank her because during those strange times she thought to do the most important thing of all.

She wrote everything down.

Eva Rice
February 2006

C2242

ACKNOWLEDGMENTS

I must first of all thank my granddaughter, Eva Rice, who set these diaries on their first step to publication.

I would also like to thank Claire Paterson of Janklow and Nesbit, my agent, Susan Watt and Mark Johnson, my editors at HarperCollins, Sacha Bonsor who helped me edit the diaries, and Caroline Boon who typed the first draft to my dictation from the diaries themselves.